"Goffee and Jones have taught us much in the last two decades about how to be outstanding leaders. And it is our job as leaders to create the distinctive cultures that will attract and foster talent and leadership. In this book, they show us how to do this, clearly demonstrating, as no one has before, the key importance of a few simple cultural traits in order for companies to be great."

—BELMIRO DE AZEVEDO, former Chairman and CEO, Sonae

"More than ever, the challenge for leaders is to build organizations that maximize the creative power of their people in a sustainable way. In this extremely relevant and practical book, Goffee and Jones challenge long-held assumptions and provide a framework and principles for bringing the ideal organization closer to reality."

—CECILE FROT-COUTAZ, CEO, FremantleMedia Ltd.

"The combination of the right products with the right people drives a brand's success. After showing that leadership is not given but earned in *Why Should Anyone Be Led by You?*, Goffee and Jones now demonstrate that to complete the equation, a leader must build and shape the right organizational culture to stimulate creativity and ensure long-term success."

—CHANTAL GAEMPERLE, LVMH Group Executive Vice President, Human Resources and Synergies

"A great sequel to *Why Should Anyone Be Led by You?* This book lifts the discussions about authentic leadership and what makes for the best possible organization to a new level. A must-read for all CEOs."

—FRANZ HUMER, Chairman, Diageo; former Chairman, F. Hoffmann-LaRoche

"A thoroughly enjoyable and enriching book. There is something profound and thought provoking on every page. I was left inspired to strive to make my company an even better place to work."

—HELEN HYDE, Personnel Director, Waitrose

"Goffee and Jones have a knack for asking the right questions at the right time. The workplace as we know it is broken, and no amount of personal, 'authentic' leadership is going to fix it. A primer on what it will take to build organizations where people can truly be their best, this book is a must-read for anyone concerned with attracting the best talent and fostering their creativity."

—HERMINIA IBARRA, professor, INSEAD; author, *Act Like a Leader, Think Like a Leader*

"If you were to design the best workplace on earth, what would it look like? You can find the answers to this question in this wonderful book. *Why Should Anyone Work Here?* is full of inspiring examples, intellectual wisdom, and practical advice on how to design an organization that brings out the best in its people. It is bound to become required reading for any senior executive."

—COSTAS MARKIDES, professor, London Business School

Why should anyone work here?

Why should anyone work here?

WHAT IT TAKES TO CREATE AN AUTHENTIC ORGANIZATION

Rob Goffee / Gareth Jones

HARVARD BUSINESS REVIEW PRESS
Boston, Massachusetts

Copyright 2015 Rob Goffee and Gareth Jones
All rights reserved
Printed in the United States of America

10 9 8 7 6 5 4 3 2 1

No part of this publication may be reproduced, stored in or introduced into a retrieval system, or transmitted, in any form, or by any means (electronic, mechanical, photocopying, recording, or otherwise), without the prior permission of the publisher. Requests for permission should be directed to permissions@hbsp.harvard.edu, or mailed to Permissions, Harvard Business School Publishing, 60 Harvard Way, Boston, Massachusetts 02163.

The web addresses referenced in this book were live and correct at the time of the book's publication but may be subject to change.

Library of Congress Cataloging-in-Publication Data

Goffee, Robert.
    Why should anyone work here?: what it takes to create an authentic organization / Rob Goffee and Gareth Jones.
        pages cm.
    ISBN 978-1-62527-509-7 (hardback)
    1. Corporate culture.   2. Organizational behavior.   3. Leadership.
    I. Jones, Gareth, 1951 August 21- II. Title.
    HD58.7.G64155 2015
    658.3—dc23   2015017103

The paper used in this publication meets the requirements of the American National Standard for Permanence of Paper for Publications and Documents in Libraries and Archives Z39.48-1992.

Dedicated to Professor John W. Hunt
A great teacher, mentor, and friend

Contents

Contents

Why
should
anyone
work
here?

Why Should Anyone Work Here?

A talented young product designer with an unusual perspective and skill set is repeatedly told that her ideas are too offbeat and she should get with the program. She starts scanning the web for other opportunities.

A smart, ambitious middle manager feels growing frustration at the poor communication of a strategy by his boss and other company leaders. How can he effectively manage his people if he doesn't know what's really going on?

An experienced marketing executive in a large consumer products company yearns for a greater sense of purpose and meaning in her work, and wonders whether it will be possible to find it at her current company.

A new employee at a large, forward-thinking professional services firm comes to work thinking about how invigorating the onboarding process has been, and how the organization will actually help *him* to reach the next level of his career.

We used to think that successful, high-performance organizations had "strong" cultures within which individuals did or did not fit. But the paradigm is changing. Organizations no longer hold all the cards, and can no longer dictate all the rules. Instead, they are finding they must increasingly adapt to the needs and desires of the people they would like to be part of their enterprise. Sustained high performance, it turns out, requires nothing less than a reinvention of the habitual patterns and processes of organizations.

What should those patterns and processes be? Imagine that you have been challenged to design the best organization on earth to work for. It's an organization that will be a beacon for attracting and retaining talent, a place that consistently brings out the very best in its people and in the business itself. What would that company be like? How would you build and sustain it?

The need for such a reimagined workplace has become increasingly urgent. Despite high unemployment in many countries, and workforces spanning an unprecedented four generations, we are in the midst of a worldwide talent shortage.[1] More than one-third of employers in a 2013 US survey reported trouble filling positions for a variety of jobs, including skilled trades workers, engineers and mechanics, salespeople, and managers and executives.[2] What's more, companies today find themselves competing not only against other firms for employees but also against talented workers' increased ability to jump the corporate ship and go solo, thanks to an array of technological advances.

Relatedly, look at companies like Yahoo, Best Buy, and Hewlett-Packard, which have swung in the direction of tighter, *less*-flexible workplaces. By battening down the hatches and summoning their web-commuters back to the office, some corporations hope to strengthen the corporate culture and social fabric, and to weed out nonproducers. But here is the challenge: if companies hope to bring their most skilled people back to the office, and continue to attract more of the best, they had better build more satisfying places to work. They had better be constantly asking themselves a tough question: *Why should anyone work here?*

Our earlier book on leadership asks a different question—*Why should anyone be led by you?*—and argues that authenticity is a necessary condition for the exercise of effective leadership.[3] Put simply, we urge current and aspiring leaders to "be themselves—more—with skill." The message has resonated broadly. But over the years since we published that book, we've often heard this response to its framing question—"I will be an authentic leader when my organization is authentic." So the ideal—or authentic—organization should allow and encourage us to be our best selves. Which brings us back to our opening question: How do you build the best workplace on earth for your people?

That's what this book is about. But before we describe the key dimensions of an authentic organization, we need to say a bit about how organizations have long been a breeding ground for inauthenticity, and how the context is changing.

Organizations and Their (Ongoing) Discontents

Let's begin with a little history. We have come a long way, indeed, from the "organization man" era of the 1950s and 1960s, in which the goal and ideal was to mold oneself to fit into the company. Think for a moment of all the talented people you know—many of whom have had "successful" careers—who would rather *not* be in large organizations, who see them as alienating, overly constraining, and depressingly conformist.

The slings and arrows of organizational life in the industrial age are well known, thanks to seminal twentieth-century thinkers and critics such as Max Weber, Joseph Schumpeter, and others. But as we've moved beyond this age into the twenty-first century, the organizational discontents have become even more starkly evident. A recent report about banking by New City Agenda concluded that banking executives have lost their moral compasses and find themselves blindly following orders.[4] HSBC, which employs 240,000 people, admits to having "an organizational bias where good people let bad things happen to survive."[5]

Many people still feel they have no real choice about where they work and the work that they do. As Emile Durkheim would have described it a century ago, we continue to live and work in a world largely characterized by a mixture of the forced division of labor, where individuals are effectively driven to allocated occupations due to existing social structures and labor market conditions, and the anomic division of labor, where economic institutions lack moral regulation.

Notwithstanding these entrenched social structures, a fundamental shift is indeed taking place all around us. The old paradigm has flipped. More and more, today's businesses find that, rather than asking or forcing individuals to step into line with the organization's needs, they must adapt and transform themselves to attract the right people, keep them, and inspire them to do their best work. What is the context driving this paradigm flip? We see four main factors.

A New World of Work

First, *capitalism is reinventing itself.* It is responding to some fundamental challenges. The most obvious is the financial crisis of 2008, when our inability to control global financial capitalism was starkly revealed. In our view, we are still far from solving the deep issues raised by the crisis regarding the purpose and structure of the corporation. (For some historical perspective, it was seven years after the Great Crash of 1929 that J. M. Keynes published *The General Theory of Employment, Interest, and Money.*) Economists are still perplexed by the crisis of 2008. What is clear is that these issues cannot be resolved by regulation alone. Organizations must rediscover their moral purpose, and the ongoing, vigorous debate around corporate governance reflects this concern. Neither the American nor the European model has proved adequate to the scale of the problem. It stands to reason, however, that if capitalism is to successfully reinvent itself, then rethinking organizations must be an important part of that reinvention. In fact, a big part of what's directly forcing the reinvention is that individuals are rethinking their relationship (or contract, if you will) with organizations. And they are not demanding less of organizations, but more—more accountability, more opportunities for self-expression and development, more transparency, more responsiveness—beyond the basic demand to earn a living.[6]

Second, *global shifts in the nature of economic power* reveal that within a few years, emerging markets such as China, India, Korea, Indonesia, Brazil, Russia, and South Africa will constitute an estimated 70 percent of world growth—with China and India alone accounting for 40 percent of that growth. Further, these facts remind us that the capitalist enterprise can take many forms. Consider, for example, that the world's fastest-growing capitalist economy, China, is under the control of the Central Committee of the Chinese Communist Party. Moreover, two of the largest banks in the United Kingdom are majority owned by the state (the economic crisis achieved what a hundred years of social democracy could not!). And Singapore, with a tremendous record of sustained growth from unpromising beginnings, looks like a quintessentially capitalist society—until you delve into the ownership structures of some its most influential organizations. There you will find the hand of the state powerfully evident.

None of this is quite what we might have expected! It's not long ago that people were predicting that liberal capitalism would dominate the world and constitute the "end of history."[7] Organizations now confront a world of complexity and diversity, where old certainties are shaken to their core. At the level of the individual,

5

that means old assumptions about employment and careers no longer hold, yet a prevalent new pattern is difficult to discern. For example, the desire to belong to a community seems as strong as ever, but the nature of that community is changing. Corporate communities, in particular, are increasingly global, multicultural, and—at least in some respects—virtual, with their memberships changing ever more frequently. This profound shift has resulted in communities that are more dynamic and diverse, and in which knowledge and power is more broadly distributed.

Third, *rates of technological and scientific change*—faster than ever before in history—have reframed the context. Nanotechnology, genetics, neurophysiology, and biotechnology will all change our world. And of course, the exponential rise of social media and the capacity of organizations to mine big data are in and of themselves major forces for radical change. Some have even argued that the "second machine age" is producing a "hollowed-out labor market" with a rapid growth of high-value, high-discretion jobs and a simultaneous growth of low-level, low-skill jobs, leaving us with a squeezed middle.[8] Life at the bottom of this occupational structure may feel very unfair. Others have gone further, claiming that platforms are replacing corporations as the focus of economic activity.[9] Although there may be cross-cultural variations in the way businesses tackle these fundamental issues, the internet means that organizations are increasingly judged by global standards. Transparency becomes not just nice to have, but rather an organizational imperative driven by the impact of technology on communications. Somewhat paradoxically, globalization has made us all both more differentiated and more connected.

Fourth, many *mature economies face a demographic time bomb:* their workers are aging, so there are practical questions about how pensions will be funded in the future. But there are also social questions: huge increases in the number of older citizens will mean a rise in medical costs to treat the physical and mental problems associated with age, such as dementia and diabetes. At the other end of the demographic scale, sustained high levels of youth unemployment may produce a disaffected and alienated generation. Without the socializing experiences of work, these young people become much more likely to develop mental health issues like depression and addiction. Even for those who find work in organizations, aspirations have changed. The research on generations shows, at the very least, that the psychological contract between employee and organization has shifted considerably. In many economies, the indications are that by 2020 Gen Y will compose around 50 percent of the workforce. Although we hesitate to generalize, what is clear is that among this cohort the organization man is dead. Younger employees are increasingly attracted to organizations whose values they can identify with. But it is not just the young—for a long time now we have known that middle-level, middle-aged managers are increasingly disenchanted with corporate spin.[10]

It is fashionable to argue that organizations are not changing as fast as their environment. But the truth is that capitalism has shown itself remarkably adept at reinvention. The move from mercantile to industrial capitalism, the rise of the joint stock company, the development of financial capitalism, the growth of international and, later, global enterprises—all are evidence of the chameleon-like quality of capitalism.

To our minds, the business organization shares this quality, and that constitutes grounds for optimism. At a fundamental level, people want to do good work in organizations in which they believe. Indeed, we subscribe to the view that the capacity for work is a species-defining characteristic. Among the higher primates, only human beings have the capacity to work in organizations and the ability to derive huge satisfaction from it. But that potential for satisfaction too often goes unrealized, at a cost both to us as individuals and to the organizations we work for.

So, what kind of organizations can deliver this satisfaction? In our last book we argued that "giving clever people the license, the freedom, the environment, the culture, the necessary discipline to express and develop their talent is success in itself . . . the challenge in the clever economy is to unleash that potential."[11] The risk, of course, is that the challenge goes unmet, the potential unrealized, and we end up with unfulfilled, restless, or even resentful individuals who are looking for a way out, and organizations that are less cohesive and strong, not to mention less effective and productive.

Who, specifically, will respond to the challenges and opportunities we have alluded to? *It can only be organizations.* But organizations themselves, of course, don't act. Rather, the world of organizations is made and remade through the actions of the individuals in them. Epicurus said that the proper subject of history is the actions of individuals operating in the real world. To put this in practical terms, organizations may not act, but they do offer opportunities and constraints. The task is to maximize degrees of freedom and eradicate unnecessary restrictions. This is a job not just for leaders but also for individuals throughout organizations. The shared agenda for all of us is to help *answer* as well as *ask* the central question of this book's title.

Why *Do* People Work Here?

Of course, people aren't literally answering that question every day and every hour that they're working, but when the question rises in the mind or when things happen at work that reveal an organization's true nature (and that of its leaders), some different core reasons or motivations emerge:

> **"I work here because I like the way we do things around here . . . I like the values . . . I like the culture."** There are those who may feel that "culture" is a rather squishy concept because aspects of it can be hard to quantify, but it has real substance. Culture is what gives a place its

distinctiveness, and as many are beginning to realize (and as this book will illustrate), it may be your one long-term source of competitive advantage. "Culture," as an answer to the question of what is the key element of organizational success, has been continuously popular ever since Peters and Waterman's *In Search of Excellence* put it on the modern map. Culture, in effect, has been a management fad that hasn't gone away—and that is because it *is* actually of foundational importance. The problem, perhaps, has been the many (and ill-advised) attempts to define "one best culture" when in fact there are likely to be many.[12] The examples and insights in this book will reaffirm just how crucial culture is to sustained organizational success, and will provide useful lessons in how to build one.

"I work here because we win . . . we are a high-performance organization." People have been telling us for years that they are attracted to winning organizations, however that is measured—be it market share, margin, or long-term growth. It is hardly surprising that employees take pride in their teams' and their organizations' success. The risk here is that we end up celebrating those who are driven to win at all costs (think Enron or certain Wall Street firms prior to the 2008 crisis). This has led us to a radical questioning of some of the conventional measures of organizational success— and the manner in which it is achieved.

"I work here because of the employer's reputation, its image, its value proposition . . . the brand convinces me this is the place to be." The "employer brand" answer is a useful reminder to think of how we appear not just to those who already work for us, but also to those who might in the future. To think, in other words, of the outside world. But as with all brands, the question becomes: Does the brand deliver? Does image match reality? Get this wrong and there will be trouble.

Remember Eli Lilly and Oraflex, Merck and Vioxx? Even some currently hip and fashionable places to work like Google and Apple are not immune to threats to their reputational capital. With the rapid rise of transparency thanks to technology—especially social media—reputation has become both more important and more fragile than we could ever have imagined.

"I work here because I get involved in a way that absorbs me, energizes me, and enables an exceptional contribution." This answer has to do with "engagement"—a term that has gained currency, sparking new debate, but that actually points to perennial issues such as motivation, fairness, trust, and the nature of the employment relationship. We are all continuously scoring our organizations on these issues, and often the results, even if only in our own minds, are disappointing.

When we shared our early thinking for this book with a senior executive from GE Crotonville, he wrote us a positive note saying that, in his view, we had taken the "engagement debate" and lifted it a couple of notches. But in fact we aren't starting with that debate at all, or with how organizations currently have or have not been able to "engage" employees.

In thinking about the best workplace on earth, we are in effect asking, How *might* organizations be? We were imagining a new kind of answer, one that the GE executive hadn't considered: *"I work here because it is the organization of my dreams."* And by "dream," we don't mean any kind of ethereal fantasy or illusion. We mean a positive ideal, the ideal of what an organization could be—an *authentic* organization.

Envisioning the DREAMS

In this book, then, we are unashamedly looking at the positive possibilities for organizations, now and in the future. Organizations are defined by recurrent interactions—of varying degrees of formality—in pursuit of a purpose. More precisely, we are seeking an answer to the question, What might "the best workplace on earth" look like? We make no apologies for this. None of the organizations we cite in this book are completely there yet—but we explore and highlight them for you because in one way or another we think they are alert to some of the challenges of the new context, and are doing well on at least one or two dimensions of the "dream" organization. None of them have it all sorted out, and perhaps one of their more attractive qualities is that most of them seem to understand that. But they are constantly striving for and trying to live up to the ideal, and their efforts at building authentic organizations are often inspirational.

For us, the key idea in workplace is "place." And arguably, in a knowledge-based or clever economy (to use our term from a recent book), this is the new task of leadership: less directly to excite others, more to orchestrate or to create environments where others can follow their own authentic obsession. Modern leadership may be as much about an authenticity of task or place as it is about the person leading and what that individual person thinks or does.

Curiously, we have known for about 150 years that people who enjoy what they do and where they work are more productive. Progressive thinkers as diverse as revolutionary socialist William Morris and enlightened capitalist William Hesketh Lever have argued that creating a great place to work releases both creativity and productivity. These themes are taken up in classic managerial theories like those of Herzberg and Maslow, which link high satisfaction with high performance. The modern manifestation of these ideas is to be found in the concept of engagement. Companies with highly engaged people outperform firms with the most disengaged—by 54 percent in employee retention, by 89 percent in customer satisfaction, and by fourfold in revenue growth.[13] And yet many organizations seem to go out of their way to make work alienating, frustrating, and unpleasant.

Consider the depressingly low rates of employee engagement around the world. According to a recent AON Hewitt survey, four in ten workers on average report being "disengaged" worldwide (three out of ten in Latin America; four in ten in the US; and five in ten in Europe).[14]

This finding resonates with our research. But instead of focusing exclusively on the sources of disengagement and dysfunction, we explored people's positive visions for organizations and how they are attempting to make these a reality. For more than four years now we have been asking people around the world what their ideal organization would be like—that is, one in which they could be their best selves.

Although individual answers varied widely of course, we found that the responses grouped naturally around six broad imperatives, which just happen to form a handy mnemonic:

- Difference—"I want to work in a place where I can be myself, where I can express the ways in which I'm different and how I see things differently."

- Radical honesty—"I want to know what's really going on."

- Extra value—"I want to work in an organization that magnifies my strengths and adds extra value for me and my personal development."

- Authenticity—"I want to work in an organization I'm proud of, one that truly stands for something."

- Meaning—"I want my day-to-day work to be meaningful."

- Simple rules—"I do not want to be hindered by stupid rules or rules that apply to some people but not others."

These attributes can often run counter to traditional practices and habits in companies, and they're not easy and simple to realize or implement. Some conflict with one another. Almost all require leaders to carefully balance competing interests and to rethink how they allocate their time and attention. Of course, few if any organizations possess all six virtues—and even if they did, it would be quite a feat for them to excel at all six.

We took these findings from our research with individuals and tested them against organizations that we were working with or in which we had research interests. Our focus has always been to connect the personal with the organizational (for further details, see the appendix and acknowledgments). Organizations must forge forward in the direction of this ideal or risk being left behind, competitively and by their own people in terms of engagement and commitment. We offer our findings, therefore, as a challenge: an agenda for leaders and organizations that aim to create the most productive and rewarding working environment possible.

Challenges to Overcome

On the surface, the DREAMS qualities or imperatives may seem obvious. After all, who would want to work in the opposite kind of place—an organization where conformity is enforced, where employees are the last to know the truth, where people feel exploited rather than enriched, where values change with the seasons, where work is alienating and stressful, and where a miasma of bureaucratic rules limits human creativity and effectiveness?

And yet we find that very few organizations fully illustrate even half of the qualities of this ideal workplace. Why? Our research indicates that when companies do try to tackle these issues, they do so superficially. They apply Band-Aids to problems when they arise and seem unprepared to address some fundamental underlying issues, which loom large indeed. Nineteenth-century social theory—exemplified in the works of Marx and Weber—teaches us that two great forces have shaped the modern world: the rise and domination of capitalism and the seemingly inexorable rise and power of the bureaucracy. Marx accurately predicted that capitalism would penetrate all corners of the world economy, and Weber gloomily predicted that mankind would be trapped in an "iron cage of his own making from which he could not escape"— and the iron cage was the bureaucracy.

Of course, no individual company can change all the destructive dynamics that capitalism hath wrought. But if we are to create truly authentic organizations, we cannot hide from these negative manifestations of capitalism or the dehumanizing consequences of bureaucratization. What we can do is respond to the context, one person and one organization at a time. And note: quick fixes won't work—creating or becoming a DREAMS organization means building a culture where these qualities are organic, part of the natural way of being, thinking, and acting. That is not an easy task; it's a long-term goal.

Let's begin with *difference*. We recently worked with an organization that had produced a 142-page booklet called "Managing Diversity." (We wonder how many people will actually read it.) And yet in all those pages the crucial argument that creativity (a key index of performance) increases with diversity and declines with conformity is never really made. For many organizations, accommodating differences translates into this concern with "diversity," usually defined according to the traditional categories such as gender, race, age, and religion. These are, of course, of tremendous importance, but the executives in our research were after something subtler and harder to achieve—an organization that can accommodate differences in perspective, habits of mind, core assumptions, and worldviews, and then go beyond accommodation to create a place where difference is celebrated and even leveraged to add value. Get difference right and you are rewarded with higher levels of commitment, innovation, and creativity.

What about *radical honesty*? Organizations are increasingly recognizing the importance of communications—both internally and to wider stakeholders. For example, we now find communications professionals at or near the summit of organizations. This is a step in the right direction: we have learned that reputational capital is becoming more and more important for high performance, even as that capital becomes increasingly fragile. Arthur Andersen was destroyed in a month in the wake of the Enron scandal. More recently, iconic firms like Apple, Nike, and Amazon have come under critical scrutiny for their employment practices.

And yet, the growth of the communications profession is actually more evidence that companies are taking a superficial approach to disseminating the critical information that people need to do their jobs. Why? Because so many communications professionals remain stubbornly connected to an old-world mind-set in which information is power and spin is their key skill. Surely information is power, but companies no longer have control of it. In a world of WikiLeaks, whistle-blowing, and freedom of information, their imperative should be to tell the truth before someone else does. When they do, they will begin to build long-standing organizational trust—both inside and outside the organization.

How can organizations create *extra value*? Elite organizations and professions—the McKinseys, Johns Hopkins Hospitals, and PwCs of this world—have been in the business of making great people even better for a long time now. Part of their pact with employees is, "Join us and we will develop you." Unfortunately, they deal with only a tiny proportion of the workforce. What about the rest of us? Our research shows that high performance arises when individuals all over the organization feel they can grow through their work—adding value as the organization adds value to them. That means the administrative assistants and cashiers as well as the executives and the shift managers. This is not impossible. If a company like McDonald's UK finds it profitable to train the equivalent of six full classes of students every week to attain formal qualifications in math and English, surely other companies can do more.

What does it mean for an organization to be *authentic*? This is a big question. It is fair to say that the concept of authenticity runs through *all* of the characteristics of the DREAMS organization—because authentic organizations encourage you to be your best self at work and to perform at your best. But for looking at authenticity as an individual, specific organizational quality, we have developed three markers. First, a company's identity is consistently rooted in its history. Second, employees demonstrate the values the company espouses. And third, company leaders are themselves authentic. Where this happens employees enjoy a sense of purpose, pride in what they do, and higher levels of trust. This is clearly not simple to achieve. Sadly, rather than rise to the challenge, in many organizations the task of building authenticity has collapsed into the industry of mission-statement writing. Some of the people we interviewed despaired that their company's mission statement had been rewritten for the fourth time in three years! Not surprisingly, this produces not high performance but deep-rooted cynicism.

The search for *meaning* in work is not new. There are libraries full of research on how jobs may produce a sense of meaning—and how they can be redesigned in ways that produce "engagement." But meaning in work is derived from a wider set of issues than those narrowly related to individual occupations. It also emerges from what we have called the three Cs—connections, community, and cause. Employees need to know how their work connects to others' work (and here, too often, silos get in the way). They need a workplace that promotes a sense of belonging (which is increasingly difficult in a mobile world). And they need to know how their work contributes to a longer-term goal (problematic, when shareholders demand quarterly reporting). If these deeper issues are not addressed, faddish efforts at increasing engagement will have only fleeting effects.

Finally, the truly authentic organization has *simple rules* that are widely agreed upon within the company. Many organizations display a form of rule accretion, where one set of bureaucratic instructions begets another, which seeks to address the problems created by the first set. In response to this, organizations have attempted a kind of radical delayering. This at least attempts to address the problem of losing good ideas and initiatives in a byzantine hierarchical structure. But that, too, is only a superficial fix. The ideal company is not a company without rules. It is a company with clear rules that make sense to the people who follow them, and it remains ever vigilant about maintaining that clarity and simplicity—a much larger challenge with a far greater payoff. Good rules maximize discretion which, in turn, facilitates problem solving. They unleash initiative rather than suppress it.

What to Expect from This Book

In this book we openly challenge you to build the best workplaces on earth. It's true that at the end of the day, the leaders at the top of organizations must shoulder the major responsibility for creating them. But it is just as true that creating a DREAMS organization must involve employees at all levels of work, and the themes we will discuss—relating to fundamental aspects of organizational life such as self-expression, meaningful work, and honesty—are matters of importance for everyone who works, everywhere around the world. Thus, this book is for current leaders, those who aspire to leadership, and all those individuals who strive to make organizations better places to work wherever they may sit. In other words, this book is for *you*.

So, we are optimistic but not starry eyed. The challenges are huge. There will always be reasons *not* to act; to push the pursuit of "dreams" down the list of priorities. The logic of capitalism is inevitable—so expect everything from disruptive new entrants and game-changing technologies to cheaper alternatives and pressures on costs.

But, crucially, this is not a matter of either/or. Building better workplaces is not an alternative to, but rather a means for, responding to the new challenges of capitalism, for building productivity, unleashing creativity, and winning.

Listen to these people we encountered during our research who addressed the question: "Why should anyone work here?" They give us reasons to be hopeful.

> "We build some of the most beautiful buildings on earth—and yet we do it while we enhance the environment. What could be better?" (a structural engineer)

> "My job is to make it easier for people to live with diabetes—to have full lives, raise families, ride bikes!" (a pharma salesperson)

> "A year ago I didn't have a job. Now I've grown new skills, feel like I make a contribution, and our restaurant has won a customer service prize. We are all so proud." (a fast-food service worker)

How do you create workplaces where you and your colleagues feel like this?

Many of us, sometimes seemingly against all odds, are often able to eke out meaning from the work tasks we perform—no matter how humble and restrictive they may appear. Most people want to do good work, and when it comes to *individuals' jobs,* they can often find a way to make them meaningful. But where there is almost universal criticism and pain, where positive meaning and possibility are actually degraded, is in the *organizational context*—the needless bureaucracy, the distortion of information, the politics and the silos, the intolerance of difference, the failure to help or develop those who most need it, and the pursuit of profit at almost any cost.

So though work *tasks* may give intrinsic meaning, the question for many really is: Must it be *here*? Why should I work *here*?

Whichever organization you are part of—and wherever you are within it—our aim is to inspire you to create a positive answer to this difficult question.

A quick map of how we'll proceed. In chapters 1–6 we take a closer look at each of our six DREAMS dimensions. Within each attribute we will show and discuss the advantages of succeeding and the dangers of failing—common pitfalls and some successful strategies. Each of these chapters also includes a short diagnostic instrument to help you see how your organization rates on each dimension and where you might begin your efforts to improve. We have used these questions in our research and they help to show how different response patterns can shape distinctive organizational interventions. A guide for using the diagnostic is also included in the appendix. Additionally, each of the six DREAMS chapters concludes with a list of specific Action Points for Leaders.

Chapter 7 is about helping you embark on the path toward creating and sustaining an authentic organization. We discuss how to assess just where you and your organization are, and what the key challenges are. We look at the complex pattern of trade-offs that you as a leader may have to make in customizing the six aspirations to the real context of your organization. We know of no organization that can do it all at once—therefore prioritization is key. It is inevitable that certain tensions will arise, and we offer some advice on how to deal with them.

In the conclusion we issue a rallying call to individuals and organizations to take up the challenge of building authentic workplaces. In fact, we really have no choice—the number of people all over the world who will demand this authenticity as the price of their talent and spirit will only continue to grow.

So let us begin with an exploration of how companies can encourage and celebrate people's individual differences for the betterment of the whole organization.

Chapter 1

Let People Be Themselves

Amplifying Difference Instead of Minimizing It

Look around your organization, at the people with whom you interact every day. What do you see? Does your workplace reflect a relative balance of males and females in leadership positions? A healthy range of diversity in terms of age, skin color, religious conviction, culture, or/and sexual orientation? Yes? Before you congratulate yourself on how diverse your workplace is, what if we told you it might not be diverse *enough*—or at least not in the ways that matter most?

To attract the best people and succeed as a business, the authentic organization of the future will need to foster environments where creativity and innovation are at a premium, employees feel engaged and committed, and leadership pipelines are carefully cultivated for future success. In our research, workplaces with those qualities look for an unusual kind of diversity, hiring people for differences that are more than skin deep. Differences in thought processes, frames of references and skills, among other things.

Case in point: Back in the 1980s, the business division of a US publisher had one of the most widely diverse workforces we've heard about. We think you'll agree. One senior editor had been part of a Washington think tank and was an expert on Asian culture; another held a PhD in American history; another had worked as a speechwriter for a US president and was an environmental activist. There was also an associate editor who had interned at the *New Yorker* magazine and another who had a background in foreign affairs. Only two of those editors held MBAs—and this was the business division!

Why the unusual staffing? The head of the division was an accomplished business author and thinker who understood that the best ideas wouldn't necessarily come from other business writers, or from people who looked at the world in the same ways he did, and he hired his staff accordingly. Weekly meetings of this division inevitably turned into dynamic brainstorming sessions and rapid-fire idea exchanges. There was lots of laughter but also frequent and open disagreement. Because people's individual gifts were celebrated and their limitations accepted, they felt free to raise "stupid" questions without censure. This was important; people were allowed to be who they were, and therefore an exceptional clash of ideas, knowledge, and experience occurred. Phrases like "What does that mean?" and "Educate me" were often heard, as was the occasional expletive or passionate exchange. Between meetings editors gathered informally on couches in the reception area to toss around ideas or discuss a manuscript in development.

Together, the people in this division produced some of the most innovative and cutting-edge publications for executives at the time. And it so happened that the majority of the division was white and male (this was the 1980s, remember).

While we don't recommend hiring staffs made up exclusively of *any* one particular gender or racial ethnicity or sexual orientation, etc., our point is that a different kind of diversity also needs consideration, one that goes beyond external qualities. Organizations that foster authenticity hire people *because of* (not in spite of) their differences in thinking, in the range of ideas that they bring to the table. Sometimes that kind of difference in thought and orientation in a workplace coincides with differences in race, gender, and such—but not always.

Differences—Not Just Diversity

So let's be clear about what we mean by "difference." While many companies define difference along the lines of traditional diversity categories—gender, race, age, ethnicity—the executives we interviewed were after something subtler. Like the business book division head in our example, they surrounded themselves with people whose differences in perspectives, habits of mind, and core assumptions would challenge and push them in new directions. For the purposes of this book, therefore, we will focus on *the fundamental differences in attitudes and mind-set between one person and another* (whether or not there's also a demographic difference between them).

Make no mistake: companies that succeed in nurturing people's uniqueness and individuality may have to forgo some degree of organizational process and structure. Consider the route taken by Ilkka Paananen, the CEO and cofounder of the Finnish gaming company Supercell. "We don't have an HR function, and that is a deliberate decision," he told us. "Retaining the culture and hiring the best people is our primary task . . . You cannot delegate that responsibility to HR."

Conversely, pursuit of predictability leads to a culture of conformity, what Emile Durkheim called mechanical solidarity—"a solidarity *sui generis* which, born of resemblances, directly links the individual with society." But cultures in the companies we followed were forged out of "organic solidarity"—which, Durkheim argued, rests on the productive exploitation of differences.[1] "Organic solidarity thus consists in the ties of co-operation between individuals or groups of individuals which derive from their occupational interdependence within the differentiated division of labour."[2]

There are two aspects of individuality that we'd like to explore in the context of organizations. The first, simply put, is that authentic workplaces allow people to be themselves: to have a voice, exercise discretion, express disagreement, show what they really care about, feel "natural" or self-fulfilled on the job. So we are talking not just about the buttoned-down financial services company that embraces the IT guys in shorts and sandals, but also the place where nearly everyone comes in at odd hours while accommodating the one or two people who prefer a nine-to-five schedule.

The second, equally important aspect of individuality is that effective organizations are willing and able to *leverage* the wide range of differences among their people. This is critical in fostering a culture of authenticity, and executives in our research cited this trait again and again as key to job satisfaction.

For example, the vice chancellor at one of the world's leading universities liked to stroll around campus late at night to locate the research hot spots. A tough-minded physicist, he expected to find them in the science labs. But to his surprise, he discovered them in all kinds of academic disciplines—ancient history, drama, the Spanish department. The ideal organization, then, is aware of dominant currents in its culture, work habits, dress code, traditions, and governing assumptions but—like the chancellor—makes explicit efforts to transcend them.

In this chapter we will look at examples that demonstrate how the celebration of people's differences leads to more robust organizations with more fulfilled employees. Such companies, however, are relatively rare. We therefore devote part of this chapter to exploring the sociological underpinnings of why conformity is the default for most firms. Finally, we offer a diagnostic to help you determine how well your own workplace leverages people's differences, followed by suggestions for how organizations can improve and a list of specific action points for leaders.

Walking the Talk

Consider the following three workplaces: a cluster of shops and cafes in a small Italian town; a hip, successful record label in Manhattan; and the British Army. Although most people would be hard-pressed to find a clear similarity among these seemingly incongruous contexts, our research into organizations has shown us how these three workplaces resemble one another in one crucial way: they all tap the full range of people's knowledge and talents. Indeed, it's precisely the *differences* among the people who work in these settings, their unique traits and individuality, that contribute to the success of those workplaces. (Yes, even in the army—as we will show.)

Let's begin with the cluster of shops in the Italian town, where one lucky member of this writing team (Rob Goffee) has an apartment. It's no wonder that he and his wife return to Italy as often as possible. When they walk into the local delicatessen, the owners greet them with a kiss on each cheek. They ask about the Goffees' children and tell them about theirs. They complain about the weather, no matter what it is. They talk about how things are going on their farm where their fresh meat is sourced, and they offer the Goffees samples of a new cheese. It won't surprise you that the Goffees are regular customers there.

Later in the day the Goffees enjoy a meal in the local pizzeria. When they try to pay with a credit card, the owner, Enrico, reminds them his business is cash only. Unfortunately, the Goffees have just spent their last euro on the sumptuous new cheeses at the deli. "No worries," Enrico says, shrugging his shoulders. "See you next time." You won't be surprised that the Goffees are regular customers here, too.

That evening in the town bar, they strike up a conversation with Cristina as she serves them drinks. Like them, she's a soccer fan, and a pretty passionate one. They begin to discuss the Italian league. Will Siena have a good season? Is there any chance of getting tickets? Cristina thinks they are out of luck with big games, so she starts searching the local newspaper for matches among the smaller teams. Then she provides the Goffees with detailed directions to the grounds and the best local bar there. You won't be surprised to know that Cristina's place also has a warm spot in the Goffees' hearts.

The next morning they are due to fly home, but discover their budget airline insists that passengers print their boarding passes in advance or face an exorbitant fee at the airport. Sadly, the Goffees have no printer. *Una problema*, as the Italians would say. As it turns out, Rob also needs a new briefcase, so they stop by a local upmarket leather shop, where the Goffees share their airline woes with the manager, Annetta. She immediately pulls the shutters to close the shop, takes them through the back to her office, accesses their tickets online and prints them. Rob also finds the perfect briefcase. They leave missing their Italian town already!

This is not simply the story of a delightful stroll through a Tuscan town. At one level, the story offers good examples of traders who enrich the customer experience—the friendly greeting and conversation at the deli; the pay-me-later pizzeria; the helpful bar staff; the offer of a printer at the upscale leather shop. But there is more going on than that. This story is about people expressing their individuality, their interests and passions. In doing so, they transform the "customer experience"—not just for the Goffees—from a mere instrumental economic exchange to a more personal interaction. Their interests include you. By just being who they are, they allow their customers to relax and be themselves too.

Great organizations are just like this. In great organizations, individuals do more than merely fulfill role obligations. In each example from the Italian town, people went beyond what we might expect from their roles. They brought *themselves* to their jobs and roles. And that is the kind of behavior that comes naturally in authentic organizations.

Which raises the question: What makes us like or appreciate certain places? Italy has many lovely things—sun, wine, great food, fascinating history, and fabulous architecture. But stroll up to this Italian hill town and you will also find gaggles of friends and families just relaxing and having coffee in the town square, discussing football, politics, and the weather. The appeal of the place is more than just the rolling hills and beautiful buildings; it's the *people* who infuse it with energy and character. The town is authentic and it is the people who make it so. There is no sense of it trying to be something it isn't. This also is true of places not normally considered idyllic vacation spots. Think of hard-working industrial cities such as Pittsburgh or Birmingham, England, or Oporto, Portugal. The Portuguese even have a saying that captures this distinctiveness: "Lisbon plays and Oporto works." And the fact is that, like organizations, all great towns and cities—places where you would like to work and live—communicate a sense of authenticity through people expressing their unique character.

The second workplace in our list, the cool record label, is housed in an office building on Lafayette street in the middle of Manhattan, near the Bowery—not the most fashionable area. The office is on the top floor of a tenement building with grilles over the windows to stop objects from being thrown in. One of us (Gareth) used to visit this office when he worked for the label's parent company. He recalls the first time he entered the office, feeling somewhat self-conscious in his formal blue suit. The open-plan office was noisy, highly interactive, and a little edgy. Immediately the intoxicating wave of energy hit him. Beneath the only

two windows in the loft was an area styled as a Jamaican beach party in full swing, where people hung out and talked music and artists. Within an hour, Gareth knew that if they offered him a job as the mail boy, he'd take it.

But then a dispute broke out: Which single should be the first track released off an album? Two executives engaged in a heated discussion, and tempers rose. The passion was palpable, and, fearing a fistfight, Gareth nearly intervened, pulling his weight as "senior suit." But things calmed down just in time, and later that day he found the two protagonists laughing and joking with each other. After their sharp exchange, they had devised a novel strategy for releasing a single from the album. Because that's just how things work around there.

This story is about Island Records. The label has a prolific history characterized by breaking new ground, cross-fertilizing genres, and taking risks with innovative artists. And it has been a huge commercial success. It is the label of Bob Marley, PJ Harvey, and U2. But to be clear, the label's consistently high levels of creativity and innovation are accompanied by high levels of conflict, passion, and heated exchanges. The people at Island are not cool clones kitted out in music garb by central casting. They are individuals who really care about music and about their artists. These are also individuals investing themselves in their roles, but unlike the shopkeepers in the Italian hill town, they are not producing sweetness and light. Rather, the inherent differences among them generate conflict, which feeds creativity and high engagement. And while most organizations would say they want creativity and innovation, what they often don't understand is that this typically involves passionate conflict, edgy relationships (think Lennon and McCartney), and indeed, regular failure. Perhaps one of the most contradictory organizational aspirations of recent times is, "Be innovative, but don't fail."

Which brings us to the third workplace we mentioned earlier: the British Army, in which Terry, one of Gareth's relatives, serves. The youngest of nine, Terry left an inner-city London school with few if

any formal qualifications. His prospects looked bleak. Work was hard to find, unemployment rates were high, and the economy was in the doldrums. Then he got a break— an interview to join the army. The selection process was tough and thorough, focusing on character as much as characteristics. He got in, and that's when his transformation began. Within a year, he had become fitter and stronger and had seen service in Africa, Latin America, and mainland Europe— tough experiences for anyone. The civil war in Sierra Leone, he tells us, will never leave him. He was put in a position where he had to make big decisions on which life and death hung, all while holding to the highest standards of military code, and far away from the support of a big organizational headquarters. Terry's background may be humble but his achievements have proven significant. He is now a regimental sergeant major with a deep and detailed knowledge of military procedures, and he cares passionately about his work.

What does the story of a British army recruit's career have to do with the authentic workplace we are describing in this book? On the surface, the answer might seem to be, "Nothing." One rather stereotypical view of the army is that it embodies old-fashioned hierarchical notions of leadership. But we've come to believe that the most effective armies are far ahead of many commercial organizations in leadership development. Why is this so?

First, from Terry's story, we can see that he gets early leadership experience, while many traditional organizations make people wait too long to take on leadership roles. And yet effective leadership development rests upon rich, early, and diverse experiences. Second, the armed forces recognize that leadership may be found in many different places, and a leadership pipeline needs to be full of many different kinds of people. Military organizations recognize that the moment they move into action, they cannot rely simply on the power of hierarchy. They will need leaders throughout the organization.

Contrast that example with a large consumer packaged-goods company with which we work. Its top seventy executives—who

are superficially different in that they were drawn from all over the globe—are all urbane, sophisticated, multilingual, diplomatic, and mildly humorous. In other words, *they are exactly like each other*, and that has caused problems for the organization. Their unique personal differences, which might have formed the basis of leadership ability, have been polished out of existence by the professional leadership development processes of the organization. The result is a group of executives that doesn't rock the boat, doesn't question procedures, doesn't let their individual gifts shine. The company is also struggling with its leadership pipeline—the straight-and-narrow path to the top means that too few of its middle-ranking executives have had experience out of their functions or regions.

Terry's story in the army illustrates how rich leadership pipelines (critical in the military and, we would argue, in any organization) require many different kinds of people. The best military organizations, in fact, seek to meld rigid adherence to high minimum standards with expression of creative difference. Likewise, the strongest organizational leadership pipelines rest on the recognition and cultivation of individuality.

As we've seen in our three workplace examples, self-expression, individuality, and diverse experience all can potentially garner many positives: high engagement with one's role or job, which also fosters a rich customer experience; creativity and continual innovation; and a robust leadership pipeline. These are all attributes found in what we call authentic workplaces, where people's differences are valued and leveraged—something many contemporary organizations claim that they seek. So why, then, do so few deliver?

To Conform or Not to Conform?

Let's not be utopian here. The forces for conformity in organizations are very strong, and conformity turns out to be

perfectly normal behavior for human beings. In his wonderful book *The Human Group*, US sociologist George Homans suggests several underlying human characteristics that bias us toward conformity—such as the fact that we tend to like people who are like us, and that most of us seek to avoid conflict.[3]

It could be argued, in fact, that a degree of conformity is a necessary and defining characteristic of all organizations, from families to corner stores and medium-sized businesses to giant global corporations. So what we are proposing is not a naive form of organizational anarchism. Successful individuals recognize the imperative to conform enough to generate organizational traction and connect with coworkers. If you fail this test, you quickly become labeled a maverick with little chance of achieving great things. Think about the rich literature on the first hundred days of new chief executives. One of the absolutely critical success factors is their ability to connect.

But it is important to recognize how organizations work to suppress people's individuality, both systematically and inadvertently. Competence models (hugely popular over recent years), for example, are a deliberate attempt to narrow the range of differences in terms of appropriate capability. In effect, they signal the aptitudes, skills, and motives regarded as "appropriate," which are then carefully measured and rewarded. The message is clear: fit within these boxes or go elsewhere. If competence models are too prescriptive and mechanically applied, they become mechanisms for mind-numbing conformity. The same can be said for appraisal systems, "management by objectives," and tightly defined recruitment guidelines.

Think, too, about the elaborate induction programs developed by world-class global companies. They are created with the best of intentions—to provide early networks, teach organizational norms, inculcate values, and provide recipes for success. And yet, if these organizations aren't careful, their programs quickly collapse into something close to thought reform. Instead of becoming

vehicles for expressing individuality, they, too, turn into processes generating conformity.

The problem of conformity also crops up in measurement systems, especially in big organizations. They tend to measure what's most easily measurable—for example, how many employees are of a particular race or gender. Understandably, subtle differences of perspective and mind-set get lost in such categorical definitions of "diversity." This explains why many of the executives we spoke to were intensely irritated by "tick-box approaches" to the diversity agenda, and by thick company manuals outlining how executives should manage diversity.

Note that this pathology isn't restricted to the old guard like GE and IBM. It can threaten even young, hip companies like Google and Apple. Smallness doesn't inoculate you against pressures to conform. In fact, small, often family-owned and -controlled companies can produce high levels of conformity, places where it's either the owner's way "or the highway."[4]

Less directly, "strong" corporate cultures—widely celebrated in the business literature as a vehicle for business success—strengthen shared values and behaviors but run the risk of eliminating valuable differences.[5] Think of most Western companies, where everyone is expected at work in the morning, even though some people don't begin to do their best thinking until midafternoon and evening. Conformity also results from the well-researched tendency for organizations to recruit in their own image.

For example, after Unilever had underperformed for more than a decade, it promised shareholders it would change. Unfortunately, its "new" strategy was to become world class at recruiting only people who fit in, or else promoting people from within its own ranks. Unilever executives are personable and clever—hardworking, but not workaholics. We have often mused that if we were ever shipwrecked we'd like to be marooned with Unilever people—soon the whole island would be well-organized and peaceful. We might even all meet together for sundowners! Life

would be consensual—but the resulting lack of dissent would have its consequences.

Unilever's cultural difficulties in engaging with novel ideas and innovation, therefore, did little to improve its outlook. To the company's credit, in 2009, Unilever decided to try something truly different by bringing in an outsider as its CEO. The appointment of Paul Polman testifies to Unilever's willingness to introduce change at the top. Polman had previously left a lengthy career at P&G to go to a competitor, Nestle—a rare move in an industry where company secrets are tightly guarded. With his appointment to Unilever, Polman, a larger-than-life character with a diverse set of interests (including corporate sustainability, marathon running, climbing with the blind, and 1960s acid bands), breathed new life into a historically conservative company. He also addressed its relationships with the external world. His strong criticisms of the finance community drew widespread interest; he quickly withdrew quarterly guidance to the market; and a while later he ceased quarterly profit reporting. He also strove to make Unilever more transparent in its operations (Oxfam was invited to report publicly on Unilever's supply chain in Africa). His appointment was followed by a number of external recruits into top positions, including CFO and a new chief supply chain officer but, more important, he reenergized the senior leadership cadre, which ultimately helped to turn the company around. According to one of his senior colleagues, "We can really feel the change now—he has both understood the culture and shifted it. We still feel connected to the past, but with a clear direction to the future."

Note that pressures to conform can be quite subtle. We recently consulted with a very successful global metal manufacturer. At its annual senior executive conference we noticed a highly sociable atmosphere. An extensive range of games and competitions had been organized before dinner that the participants entered with gusto, amid laughter and frivolity. A long and noisy dinner ensued, including several speeches punctuated with irreverent humor. The evening culminated in a very long session in the bar. The following morning we asked the executives—slightly worse for wear—to tell us the rules of survival and success in their organization. Unanimously the number-one rule was "be in the bar." Superficially, the slightly irreverent character of the organization and the free expression of humor suggest a tolerance for the expression of individuality. But imagine the introvert who would rather not "be in the bar" and hates organized games. Differences in personality and temperament might not be so easily accepted in that company.

Moreover, in most workplaces, the pressure to conform spans organizational ranks. Among lower-paid staff, it is almost ubiquitous. Here is where people often find themselves in "low-discretion roles" and when they are new, naturally feel motivated to be accepted in the culture. If they stay in low-discretion roles, they become habituated to them, and can end up using the company rules as a way to avoid true problem solving—becoming the petty bureaucrat of the customer's nightmare.

Similarly, employees in the middle, who are often striving to move up the corporate hierarchy, feel great pressure to fit the prevailing mold. A common mistake among people trying to acquire the relevant cultural capital is to lose their own distinctive characteristics— the very qualities and traits that helped them rise to the middle in the first place. They start to "keep their head down," "cover their backs," "do just enough," "become invisible"—all fatal to their leadership expression. Perhaps the quintessential tragic play of the twentieth century is Arthur Miller's *Death of a Salesman*, in which Willy Loman confuses his personal identity with his organization's identity. And when his organization doesn't love him anymore, he doesn't think he's a man—and he dies. The speech at the graveside is perhaps one of the most moving orations of modern drama. The alienation of the midlevel executive is also eloquently captured in William White's classic, *The Organization Man*, and David Riesman et al.'s *The Lonely Crowd*.

And then of course there's that small and perhaps rather too-exclusive group that sometimes appears in the top positions of organizations. Our work consulting to the boards of large European businesses has shown us that even very high-achieving, strong-minded, nonexecutive board directors find it difficult to express their differences without fear of being seen as "disloyal." A recent analysis of corporate governance in the United Kingdom confirmed a central issue for these directors: balancing the need to challenge executive directors with the need to also offer them support.[6] The irony is these directors are often explicitly recruited—using expensive headhunters—to bring to the board different but complementary experience and expertise. These are all "high-discretion roles," but their inability to effectively voice their difference is a regular cause of personal dissatisfaction.[7] It is also arguably a major reason why many of the boards supervising financial service corporations failed so spectacularly in their governance responsibilities during the economic crash. The problem is made worse—in our experience—by executive director board members who (with a sometimes misplaced sense of loyalty) fall in behind the CEO's position whenever they become subject to nonexecutive or shareholder scrutiny. Again an opportunity for the airing of difference is lost.[8]

As destructive as it can be, however, as humans we continue to be driven by the desire to fit in, or so Homans tells us. Apart from our tendency to like people who are like us, and the fact that most people seek to avoid conflict, Homans offers a third, more complex reason for our conforming natures—"proximity encourages similarity." Writing in the early 1950s, Homans put it in his own distinctive way: "For one reason or another, you associate with someone for a period of time; you get used to him; your behavior becomes adjusted to his, and his to yours; you feel at home with him and say he is a good fellow . . . You can get to like some pretty queer customers if you go around with them long enough."[9]

Homans is reminding us that individuals are not the passive recipients of organizational attempts to make them conform.

They are in fact coconspirators, seeking conformity as a way of minimizing personal risk and discomfort. And yet, as extensive research has shown, there are clear personal and organizational benefits when people feel free to be who they really are.[10] So individuals and organizations alike will have to consciously push against the magnetic draw of conformity if they hope to reap those benefits.

What Organizations Can Do

During the course of our research we developed a diagnostic for identifying an authentic organization, what we think of as a "dream company," and we report on this data throughout this book and in the appendix. We are encouraged to find that some organizations have made real strides in this area. As we've said, when a person is able to express his or her uniqueness, both the individual and the organization win. The sidebar—"How Much Does Your Organization Value Your Individuality?"—offers a diagnostic that we used to assess organizations' ability to support people's individuality and differences.

In the responses to these questions that we received from senior executives, we noted that they were least satisfied on two items: "We are all encouraged to express our differences" and "People who think differently from most do well here."[11] Counterintuitively, lower-level participants often reported most positively the item "I am the same person at home as I am at work." This finding is not easy to interpret. As we show below in one of our examples (Waitrose), the response can be connected with high levels of positive work engagement. But sometimes, curiously, it can represent a lack of identification with the work role itself. Instead, people take their personal and community involvements to work as a means of resisting the control mechanisms they encounter. This may be connected to the low levels of engagement that are widely reported.

Diagnostic: How Much Does Your Organization Value Your Individuality?

1 = Strongly Disagree   2 = Disagree   3 = Neither Agree Nor Disagree
4 = Agree   5 = Strongly Agree

_____ I am the same person at home as I am at work.

_____ I am comfortable being myself.

_____ We are all encouraged to express our differences.

_____ People who think differently from most do well here.

_____ Passion is encouraged, even when it leads to conflict.

_____ More than one type of person fits in here.

Consider any statement to which you assign a 1 or 2 as worth your sustained attention. An overall score below 18 suggests that this area of your organizational life requires improvement. Ask yourself how long you will give the organization to make genuine progress.

Importantly, the diagnostic statements reflect the core essential dynamics that lead to and predict three advantages, in particular, that we began to explore in some of our examples thus far.

First, the level of self-expression and individuality in organizations correlates positively with high work engagement and commitment (think of the Tuscan shopkeepers). Second, that same ability to express individual differences boosts people's creativity, which fosters obvious benefits in their workplaces, not the least of which is innovation (as it did at the record label) and productivity. (Conversely—and perhaps not surprisingly, when you think about it—creativity decreases when sameness is encouraged and individuality squelched.) Third, organizations that encourage individuals to seek out new and different experiences—to be themselves more, and to gain the skills they need to do that—bolster the quality of their leadership pipeline (as does the British Army).

All of these advantages await organizations that actively recognize and nurture the differences among their people. Let's look at three specific ways in which we have seen organizations do just that—and which point to steps that other companies might take as well.

Foster High Work Engagement and Commitment

The first two phrases from the diagnostic, "I am the same person at home as I am at work" and "I am comfortable being myself," reflect the emotions of people we spoke to who were happily engaged in and committed to their jobs. Consider Waitrose, Britain's most successful food retailer of recent years—as measured by sales growth, market share, and perhaps most importantly, staff and customer loyalty. Waitrose leaders recognize that great retailing depends upon people's unique differences. Remember, this is an industry that necessarily focuses on executing operational efficiency—supply chain management, merchandising, and food safety are absolutely essential for sustained food retailing success. Waitrose is good at all of them. It is also effectively a cooperative: employees are referred to as partners; every one of them is a co-owner who shares in the company's annual profits. So the source of staff loyalty is not much of a mystery. But even so, the company goes to great lengths to draw out and support people's personal interests. If you want to learn piano, Waitrose will pay half the cost of the lessons. There's a thriving club culture for people interested in things like cooking, crafts, and swimming. We have a friend whose father learned to sail because he worked for this organization.

And yet, Waitrose builds and sustains its competitive edge by nurturing the small sparks of creativity that make a big difference to customer experience. Waitrose strives to create an atmosphere where people feel comfortable being who they are. They want people to look forward to coming to work—perhaps the best indicator that individuals are highly engaged and committed. As one senior executive told us, for some of their partners, coming to work "is their sanity." Difference is embraced in all its forms. We were told a delightful story of a shopping-cart collector with Downs syndrome who kissed the store manager every morning upon arriving to work. Even the management performance-and-assessment system is as much concerned with how things are done as it is with simple metrics. We were struck when a senior executive told us, "Friends and family would recognize me at work." Another executive explained: "Great retail businesses depend on characters who do things a bit differently. Over the years we have had lots of them. We must be careful to cherish them and make sure our systems don't squeeze them out."

High engagement also defines the privately funded London Organising Committee of the Olympic Games and Paralympic Games (LOCOG), which was charged with overseeing the planning, development, and implementation of the summer 2012 games. LOCOG set itself ambitious targets for diversity and inclusion using some conventional markers such as age, gender, ethnicity, and disability. But the approach went deeper than politically correct compliance. LOCOG CEO Paul Deighton (previously at Goldman Sachs) described the games as a unique opportunity to break down ethnic, cultural, religious, political, and economic barriers: "Diversity and inclusion is at the heart of everything we do." For example, the LOCOG Trailblazer Programme was designed to ensure that people of all ages could apply to be "early entry volunteers." In the words of Jean Tomlin, HR director, "We had retired accountants, auditors from the City, school teachers, car park attendants, skilled workers—people from all walks of life alongside paid staff—both sides learnt from each other." It became in effect, "a learning to work with difference" initiative.

One measure of LOCOG's success was revealed in an interesting statistic. After a few years working with the committee (LOCOG started its work in 2006), employees were much more likely to voluntarily declare themselves gay or lesbian in data relating to sexual orientation. Indeed, the marked increase in those numbers showed that LOCOG had successfully created a culture where, as staff member Oliver Sweeting put it, "I was allowed to be me—and could throw myself into my work in a way I had never been able to elsewhere." You can see that a clever diversity and inclusion strategy takes you to difference beyond diversity. Oliver is being his best self.

What led to LOCOG's success in crafting a workplace where people with a variety of differences could do their jobs effectively? According to Tomlin, a prime factor was absolute clarity about what kind of organization LOCOG desired, and inclusiveness was at its heart. They recruited diverse people (including the HR director herself, who is a black Briton), using a thorough induction process that stressed the tough values of diversity on which LOCOG was premised. They appointed champions (executive committee directors) for each pillar of inclusiveness, and CEO Deighton was very vocal in his public support. Directors from the senior executive team, including functions such as venues, legal, sport, and marketing, were all committed advocates. The value of inclusiveness was embedded in LOCOG's procurement processes, and it actively persuaded other sporting organizations to embrace similar values. Tomlin was adamant that there was no simple solution, but that the value of diversity had to be woven into everything the organization did. Diversity came to be seen as an asset, not as a problem.

Boost Creativity, Innovation, and Productivity

Organizations where people are encouraged to be themselves actively work to boost employees' creativity, innovation, and productivity—best exemplified by the following two statements in our diagnostic: "We are all encouraged to express our differences" and "People who think differently from most do well here." Certainly our earlier example of the book-publishing division exemplifies the positive effects of a diversely staffed team on creativity and innovation. Another example is Arup, perhaps the world's most creative engineering and design company. Many iconic buildings bear the mark of Arup's distinctive imprint—from the Sydney Opera House to the Centre Pompidou and the Beijing Water Cube. How does Arup do it? To begin with, the firm approaches its work holistically. When Arup builds a suspension bridge, for example, it looks beyond the concerns of the immediate client to the region that relies on the bridge to ensure that solutions benefit not just the client but also the society in which the solutions live. Arup's people therefore collaborate with mathematicians, economists, artists, and local politicians alike. Accordingly, the firm considers the capacity to absorb different skill sets and personalities as key to its strategy.

"We want there to be interesting parts that don't quite fit in," says chairman Philip Dilley. "That's part of my job now—to prevent the organization from becoming totally orderly."[12] Dilley adds that hiring people who don't fit the expected mold has become part of Arup's culture. "When I ran my design group, I brought in people who were experiments," he says. "We employed a mathematician that we couldn't charge to a client. He subsequently studied engineering and now he has taken us to places we'd never have gone otherwise."

Not surprisingly, conventional appraisal systems don't work in such a world. Arup doesn't use quantitative performance measurements, and it doesn't articulate a corporate policy on how employees should progress. For example, its appraisal form asks employees to list their work expectations the following year—with deliberately little guidance beyond that. The form has no structure in the "objectives" section—just a white box. Nor is there quantitative measurement in performance systems; performance is left to managers and individuals to define as they see fit. As Dilley explains: "We don't want there to be only four objectives. It means you'll never get the fifth one . . . I'm really saying to people: We would like you to do this, but do it your way and give us some pleasant surprises on the way."

Managers make their expectations clear, but individuals decide how to meet them. An overriding sense of self-determination infuses the people at Arup. "Self-determination means setting your own path and being accountable for your success," said one senior HR executive. "For this to work individuals need to feel it—from the culture rather than a 'program.'" Arup's culture therefore includes few hard-and-fast rules that affect the work that gets done or the paths that people's careers take in the firm. "Accountability is pushed to the regions and often to the individual office," the executive added. "There are no corporate views on how individuals should develop. Development and progression is your own business, with our support."

Accordingly, reward principles in Arup also recognize that progression is not always "rounded"—very senior leaders have progressed in deep rather than in broad ways. Arup awards lifelong Fellowship titles to creative and technical innovators, often in a specialty that has made them world-renowned: Tristram Carfrae, for instance, is the Arup deputy chairman behind the Beijing Water Cube swimming pool developed for the Olympics. He also happens to be a board member, and offered perhaps the best description of Arup's secret to success: "It's very organic, very chaotic. It's incredibly hard to swing the firm in a violent way. Every individual has the right of self-determination. To move them you have to persuade every single one of them. That it is a good thing for the firm to be doing and a good thing for them. Which is incredibly time consuming and incredibly frustrating. But it's a strength!"

The opportunity and challenge of nurturing a widely diverse staff as a route to innovation and creativity takes us back to our story of the record label, whose unique cast of characters set the stage for some startlingly heated creative debates. We have found the same at other companies with which we've worked, including the world's most successful pharmaceutical companies—GSK, Novartis, Roche, Novo Nordisk, and Merck Serono. These places are of course full of clever, highly rational scientists, obsessed with data and research protocols. But visit one of their research seminars where they discuss potential breakthrough compounds, and you will be shocked by the intensity of their arguments. Individuals whom we had previously, perhaps falsely, labeled as introverts suddenly become exuberant extroverts, passionately extolling the virtues of their own research. Everyone in the room seems to think himself or herself on the verge of a Nobel prize and of course, most of them are wrong. But as a senior head of R&D at one of the companies explained to us, "They absolutely must believe in the power of their own ideas—even when they are wrong!" Research scientists need to believe passionately in their ideas in the same way that record executives must believe in their artists. For the truth is that for all of the new compounds a pharmaceutical company might have in the early stages of development, very few will ever become products. Which is to say that really innovative pharma companies strive to keep the innovation funnel as wide as possible in the early stages.

LVMH, the world's largest luxury goods company (and growing rapidly), provides another example of an organization where people's differences translate into high creativity. At such a firm, you'd expect to find brilliant, creative innovators like Marc Jacobs and Phoebe Philo. And you do. Visit LVMH House, their global training center in London, and as you pass through the entrance hall, you will find the walls decorated with photos of illustrious world-class fashion designers, "chefs de cave," and "noses" from the perfume business.

But alongside these wonderful creative talents, there is a higher than expected proportion of executives and specialists who focus on monitoring and evaluating the creatives' ideas in an objective, business-focused way. One of the secrets of LVMH's success is its capacity to develop a culture where these opposite types can thrive and indeed work cooperatively with each other. The company recognizes that while people can be passionate, they also need to have a culture that acts as a vehicle for expressing that passion. There is a delicious irony about observing slightly wacky designers from haute couture or jewelry being grilled by highly numerate accountants about the sales potential of their latest obsession. Curiously, they seem to know that they need each other. Part of this comes from selection. For example, LVMH deliberately looks for creatives who want to be famous. These are much more likely to appreciate the skills of the monitors in picking ideas that have commercial potential.

Likewise, when we evaluate the effectiveness of a record company, we will note how far away the finance director is from the creative driving force of the label. If the finance function is in a building on the next block, there is probably a problem. Great record companies need the diverse talents of groundbreaking talent scouts, brilliant finance people, and sophisticated marketers—all mixing it up together. If any one type of person dominates the organization, its effectiveness and creativity inevitably are reduced. For example, some record companies allow the A&R function ("artists and repertoire"—the group responsible for finding emerging talent) to be too dominant, and what follows is a lack of commercial focus. Or more recently at EMI, the finance function became far too powerful and the company simply couldn't retain its star creative talent.

Build a Robust Leadership Pipeline

Organizations where people are encouraged to express their unique differences also cultivate a stable of potential leaders. In our diagnostic, the statements "Passion is encouraged, even when it leads to conflict" and "More than one type of person fits in here" reflect workplaces with well-tended pipelines for future organizational leaders.

Yet many so-called "leadership" pipelines are an illusion. What many of the world's most sophisticated companies really have is a "management" pipeline and, as we have already argued, these effectively produce extremely well-polished managers. In itself, there is nothing wrong with this—big organizations need managers, and lots of them. But the cry for the last decade or more has been "Why can so few act as leaders?"

Our answer has been that they have not been able—or perhaps willing—to use their personal *differences* to excite others to higher performance, which is the real task of leadership as distinct from management. The question that titled one of our previous books, "Why should anyone be led by you?" is really asking: What's *different* about you that might excite others?

So to build a successful leadership pipeline it's necessary to facilitate a process whereby individuals are able to know and show themselves enough. And that can be done only in organizations where people can realize and usefully deploy their unique or distinctive qualities in a way that can improve performance. Many large-scale, global businesses from several distinctive sectors are engaging with this issue with some success—they include, from our own experience, Unilever, Nestle, Roche, PwC, Novartis, and Heineken.

Perhaps the most unusual example we've found of hiring practices that leverage people's differences (and ultimately feed leadership channels) is the House of St Barnabas (HoSB), which runs a London members-only club with a twist: it's a nonprofit. In fact, HoSB might offer a model for the new type of "hybrid" workplace that can make the difference on many dimensions, bringing together possibly the widest range of people imaginable: high-net-worth individuals, the creative sector of Soho, and the homeless!

"You have one life. You are one person," says chairman David Evans. "There's no sense in separating—it's wrong ethically and makes no commercial sense because people work better if they can express themselves. It's tricky sometimes in our case since we are bringing together different worlds—charity and the private sector."

The history of the HoSB club (a London charity that has served the homeless since 1846) evolved yet again when Evans and CEO Sandra Schembri reopened it in 2013 as a members club with a cause: sustained employment for the homeless. This required radical and expensive action—the transformation of a slightly dilapidated London building (including a chapel) in the Soho district into a full-service club complete with bars, restaurants, meeting rooms, gardens—and decorated with the work of some of the coolest contemporary London artists. Funds came from some trusts and foundations, from social investment loans, and through the investment of a large catering company, Benugo, which effectively partnered with the charity. Surplus from the club's membership fees and revenues funds an Employment Academy for homeless participants on its charitable programs. Working only with homeless who meet certain criteria (such as being substance free), HoSB's core motto could be "from not employable—to a job."

"We ask a lot about personality when we hire and how people might fit," Schembri says. "'Tell us a random fact about yourself,' we ask. We want to signal it's OK to bring yourself to work. But at the same time they must be wedded to our cause—to want to be architects of change! They must also be prepared to tolerate differences here and to work differently. They will be working alongside graduates from our [Employment Academy] program. In an industry which is fast paced and unforgiving, they have to show patience (hard for chefs!), be comfortable with teaching others, be enthusiastic about others' potential, and understand that participants can't do everything!"

HoSB also goes out of its way to build difference into the membership as well. For example, one question for applicants is,

"What color is your personality?" Speaking of the club's "quirky" member-selection process, Schembri says: "There is induction, but not indoctrination."

The benefits of tapping the full range of people's differences—their unique knowledge and talents—may seem obvious, yet it's not surprising that so few companies do it. To put it mildly, it's very hard to do. For one thing, uncovering biases isn't easy. (Consider the assumption the diligent chancellor made when at first he equated research intensity with late-night science lab work.) More fundamentally, though, efforts to nurture individuality run up against countervailing efforts to increase organizational effectiveness by forging clear incentive systems and career paths.

We referred earlier to the dangers of pursuing predictability, which leads to the kinds of conformist cultures that Emile Durkheim warned against. Fortunately, companies like LVMH, Arup, and Waitrose, among others we've studied, are forged out of the kind of "organic solidarity" that Durkheim argued rests on the productive exploitation of differences. Why go to all the trouble? We think Ted Mathas, head of the US's largest mutual life insurance company, New York Life, explains it best: "When I was appointed CEO, my biggest concern was, would this [job] allow me to truly say what I think? I needed to be myself to do a good job. Everybody does."

In the next chapter, we will look at another organizational quality that people wish for: to know what is really going on and not have vital company information withheld from them. When you think about it, this goes hand in hand with "being yourself" in a company where your differences are acknowledged and appreciated. That is what happens in the shops in the Italian village, and it's what keeps the people in our record label example coming back to work every day. It is also what helps organizations like the British military craft robust leadership pipelines. It's all about seeing people as individuals and treating them with respect *because* of their unique differences, not in spite of them.

Action Points for Leaders

✔ **Hire for difference—in people's thought processes and life experiences, among other qualities.** In interviews, explore people's origins and backgrounds; this will illuminate how people see themselves and the world. Don't rely only on search firms—they often tend to produce lists of the usual suspects. Keep a notebook of talent that you spot in unusual places (remember the Arup example). Don't forget the familiar advice: "Hire for attitude and train for aptitude."

✔ **Don't allow HR to dominate recruitment selection and induction.** Interview people sequentially, which will allow you to collect a variety of perspectives on each candidate. If done skillfully, you will enhance your chances of discovering difference. Because your investment in people is the most important investment you'll ever make, be sure that HR involves line executives in hiring processes and makes every effort to seek out difference in new hires and protect those differences.

✔ **Be more tolerant of differences and how they are expressed.** Conventional wisdom has always been that leaders should encourage what sociologists call *cognitive* conflict—the clash of ideas—and discourage *affective* conflict—the clash of emotions. Our observations lead us to believe that in high-performance organizations, a little clash of emotions is actually no bad thing. Emotions are a major source of energy at work; build time into your meetings for the expression of individual feelings.

✔ **Nurture the difference found in "characters."** First-class customer experience depends on people exceeding their role expectations. Under the right conditions, this won't be confined to small Italian hill towns. "Characters" and other kinds of unique individuals have a place in the organization too. Reward those who go beyond the job description.

✔ **Design performance measures that allow for creative surprises and that acknowledge differences in trajectories of development.** Build slack into your organizational time to encourage experimentation. It is now clear that organizations can innovate only when individuals and teams are allowed some space to try new things. This is a technique that 3M has used for years and that Google more recently has made famous. Recognize that failure is inevitable when you experiment.

✔ **Seek a consensus around values, but allow for individual creative expression.** A key leadership task is to create organizational cohesion. The challenge, however, is to achieve this without producing homogeneity. Creativity increases with diversity, but diversity is difficult to manage. This conundrum can be solved by seeking consensus around values while allowing creativity around behavior.

Chapter 2

Practice Radical Honesty

Communicating What's Really Going On

When a wellhead on BP's Deepwater Horizon drilling rig exploded off the coast of Louisiana in April 2010, it killed eleven workers and triggered an oil spill that gushed into the Gulf of Mexico for eighty-seven days. By the time the wellhead was capped, about 200 million gallons of oil had been released into the ocean, killing generations of fish and wildlife and damaging the ecosystem.[1] Meantime, BP was widely criticized for not responding swiftly enough or, in some views, adequately acknowledging the extent of the disaster.

For example, according to one report, "CEO Tony Hayward called the amount of oil and dispersant 'relatively tiny' in comparison with the 'very big ocean.'"[2] (For one media perspective on the incident, see the sidebar, "Transparency and the BP Oil Spill.") And in a leaked e-mail sent to BP's more than eighty thousand employees, Hayward attempted to deal with the plummeting morale and attrition post-disaster.[3] Yet "the e-mail had at least one major misstep," according to one report. "Hayward trie[d] to reassure employees that they work in a safe environment and [took] aim at media reports that [said] otherwise." But with the rig explosion fresh in everyone's minds, the CEO was "fighting a losing perception battle."[4]

For organizations, engaging in such battles of perception is unavoidable. To address them, companies have built up substantial departments focused on managing external communications. But as the BP example demonstrates, managing internal communications is just as crucial, and in some companies this aspect of organizational life is indeed moving up the corporate agenda. Building authentic organizations requires nothing less than sophisticated, honest internal communications processes.

This chapter explores how practicing what we call "radical honesty" can help. As the second aspect of our ideal organization of the future, such honesty fosters loyalty, pride, and trust among employees.

We begin by defining what we mean by radical honesty, and we look specifically at the ways organizations become blocked from being completely open with employees and/or outsiders. For example, some leaders feel an obligation—as BP's Tony Hayward no doubt did—to put a positive spin on even the most negative situations, out of a best-foot-forward sense of loyalty to the organization. (Hayward subsequently stepped down as BP's CEO in July 2010.) In any case, we know that BP has focused on restoring faith with the public and employees by communicating more openly, including managing its social media sites in a more proactive way. Later in this chapter we'll explore the technological, psychological, and organizational realities that make such truth-telling in organizations imperative. Finally, as in the preceding chapter, we offer a diagnostic that will help you determine how "radically honest" your organization is, followed by suggestions for fostering open communication inside and outside of companies.

Transparency and the BP Oil Spill

"As if the worst oil spill in U.S. history along the Gulf Coast in April 2010 was not bad enough, BP added insult to injury by failing to share information with those affected and with the public at large. It ignored the social media sites where people were clamouring for the truth about what was happening. For example, BP neglected to send out any Tweets about the disaster until April 27, a week after the spill happened—an eternity in social media, by which time it was universally derided as uncaring. Josh Simpson, a comedian, created a parody Twitter account, @BPGlobalPR, and his dry Tweets were at first almost indistinguishable from the official account; it grew to 180,000 followers (compared to 18,000 for the official [BP] account today). A parody video on YouTube ('BP Spills Coffee—a very small spill on a very large table') has 11.5 million views to date. A Google search for 'BP Twitter' still has the parody Twitter account as the top search result, and, as of this writing, every link except one on the first page of results is about that parody account."[a]

a. Joanna Walters, "Timeline: Most Notorious Marine Oil Spills in History," *Telegraph*, March 23, 2014, http://www.telegraph.co.uk/earth/environment/10717493/Timeline-most-notorious-marine-oil-spills-in-history.html; Alan Mascarenhas, "BP's Global PR vs. BPGlobalPR," *Newsweek*, June 4, 2010.

Source: Excerpted from Jamie Notter and Maddie Grant, *Humanize: How People-Centric Organizations Succeed in a Social World* (Indianapolis, IN: QUE Publishing), 104–105.

What Makes Honesty "Radical"?

Our definition of radical honesty takes us a little deeper than the modern injunction for organizational transparency. We characterize it as follows: it is proactive rather than reactive; it is speedy; it surprises people with its candor; it encourages dissent; and finally, it engages with employees *and* with a wide group of stakeholders—shareholders, customers, suppliers, regulators, and the wider society. All of this requires hard work and consistent action, but also free-flowing communication. Because we live in a world where we are deluged with data, leaders and organizations need to be compelling communicators; otherwise their messages get lost in the general noise.

That is why authentic organizations find ways to unleash the flow of information, loud and clear and above the background noise. They tell it as it is, respecting employees' need to know what's really going on so that they can do their jobs. This is important for *all* organizations—large and small, public and private, complex and fast moving as well as more stable and traditional. All are now in the communications business. Increasingly, there is a shared imperative: tell the truth before someone else tells it for you!

A case in point is Google's transparency in sharing with all employees its quarterly executive team report to the board. According to Eric Schmidt, former Google CEO and now chairman:

> Your default mode should be to share everything . . . Fortunately the people running this process understand that "share everything" doesn't mean "share everything that wouldn't look bad if it leaked and that doesn't hurt anyone's feelings," it means "share everything except for the very few things that are prohibited by law or regulation." Big difference! This is why we make everyone who wants something to be removed justify exactly why it needs to come out, and the reason better be very good.[5]

The organizations we most admire, then, don't do "spin." As we were told by the many people we talked to about authentic organizations, the old world of corporate secrets is over, and organizations are still trying to catch up to this reality. There are complex social, political, and technological reasons for this dramatic change. At the social level, two phenomena coincide: first, the decline of public trust in organizations, and second, the marked decline in levels of deference to authority.[6] Politically, legislators have responded to these social changes by instituting wide-reaching "freedom of information acts" which, for all their inadequacies, have dramatically changed the information landscape. At the technological level, the explosion of social media has been transformational and means that organizations in both the public and private spheres are being forced to face new information-sharing challenges.

In any event, the old practice of "covering up" no longer works. Spin backfires. The breadth and depth of information available today has created a more knowledgeable public, less easily swayed by public relations efforts. Consider the following examples. The day after the dreadful events of 9/11, a UK government spokeswoman was revealed to have advised her colleagues that "today is a good day to bury bad news" (in nonprominent places in UK bulletins and newspapers), given the overwhelming media focus on unfolding events in Manhattan. She lost her job. Her minister lost his reputation. And the story was widely used by critics of the Tony Blair government as a damning illustration of its apparently pathological addiction to news manipulation.

More recently, the news emerged that UK retailer Tesco had sold beef burgers that contained horsemeat. The company swiftly published a public apology and promised customers that it would investigate and take any necessary action. But Tesco's public statements also carried the claim that this was a problem "for the whole food industry." Other retailers—in particular, small family butchers with direct knowledge of where their meat was locally sourced—complained. A subsequent investigation by the UK's Advertising Standards Agency led to yet more bad publicity: Tesco was publicly admonished for making a claim that, in effect, would allow it to imply this was "a problem for all retailers and suppliers." Even well-intentioned apologies can backfire.[7]

The best companies of the future, then, will practice honesty and openness as a matter of course, providing a foundation of integrity to the other five organizational qualities we explore in this book—companies where people can be themselves (which we examined in the last chapter); where people's value and strengths are magnified; where a sincere company identity pervades, rooted in authenticity; where the work feels meaningful; and where there are no stupid rules to get in the way.

Let's look now at exactly why organizations sometimes fall short of keeping information channels open.

What Blocks Radical Honesty?

This question is more complex than it looks. One illuminating theoretical take on this issue comes from the work of the German sociologist Jürgen Habermas.[8] He has developed a theory that connects power relationships in society and, indeed, in interpersonal relationships with patterns of communication. He describes how power distorts communication. For the powerful, communication becomes increasingly significant in legitimizing existing power relationships. In other words, communication becomes increasingly ideological. He also explains why power relationships at work also distort communication, to the point that honest performance-management discussions are difficult because of the power relationship among the participants. This perspective also explains why much of the information that reaches senior executives is sanitized. Power has again gotten in the way of optimal outcomes.

It would seem almost a cliché to say that organizations should be honest. So why aren't all companies more open in their communication? The barriers to candid, complete, clear, and timely communication are legion. We already mentioned how some executives (such as, perhaps, BP's former CEO Tony Hayward) feel an obligation to put a positive spin on negative events out of loyalty to the organization. Other managers see parceling out information on a need-to-know basis as important to maintaining efficiency. Still others practice a seemingly benign type of paternalism, reluctant to "worry" staff with certain information or to identify a problem before having a solution. It is of course worth noting that all organizations are political—from families to large global corporations. The issue is really whether the politics help you get things done or prevent it.[9]

At BP, the reluctance to be the bearer of bad news, especially after employee lives were lost, seems particularly poignant and deeply human. As one former BP executive told us, "There was this incredulity . . . how could this have happened?" And once the facts and extent of the damage came to light, he told us, some employees didn't want to publicly admit to working for the company.

Even so, many top executives well know that this tendency to stifle or delay news can strangle the flow of critical information. That is what happened at drug maker Novo Nordisk in the 1990s, when violations of FDA regulations at the company's Danish insulin-production facilities became so serious that US regulators nearly banned the insulin from the US market. Because of a company culture in which the executive management board was never supposed to receive bad news, CEO Mads Øvlisen learned about the situation only when it was almost too late to do anything about it. Later in this chapter we'll look at the formal steps that Novo Nordisk took to rectify the situation, but for now suffice it to say that the company had to take a long, hard look at its culture and quality-management processes.

Sometimes even "progressive" organizations have resisted openness about their workings, claiming that social and political attempts to regulate and open up companies quickly descend into a mere "tick box" farce. Our response is twofold. On the one hand, it is correct to say that crude interventions often have unintended consequences. The reforms in the Sarbanes-Oxley Act of 2002, a US regulatory attempt to make organizations more transparent to their stakeholders via the audit process, can be seen with hindsight not to have improved the process but to have deskilled it. Auditors can too easily disclaim responsibility by arguing that the question was asked and a response achieved.

On the other hand, people's desire to have timely and adequate information about the organizations that greatly affect their lives and livelihoods is undeniable and certainly hard to argue with.

Why Be Honest?

Our research has revealed a number of key reasons for companies to take seriously the call to honesty and openness in the way they conduct themselves. Perhaps not surprisingly, all of these reasons play right across the global activities of organizations, because one major consequence of globalization is that there are increasingly international standards of transparency to stakeholders. For example, the more large Asian companies are drawn into conventional capital markets rather than sovereign state funds, the more they find themselves open to global demands for information.

This is not to say that there are no cross-cultural variations in patterns of communication and expectations of transparency. But the major drivers for change are increasingly global, and are embedded in our three main reasons for companies to take seriously the call to honesty in how they conduct themselves: technological realities, human psychological needs, and organizational and regulatory changes.

Technological Realities

One of the most dramatic features of the modern world is the extent to which we are inundated with information in every possible format at every hour of the day. TV channels number in the thousands, and iPads, smartphones, and other devices combine to almost overwhelm us, as does the explosion of social media—Facebook, Twitter, and Instagram to name a few. All of this means that the old world of corporate secrets is over. As we've said, corporations have a new imperative to share the facts, or risk public exposure by someone else.

Indeed, an organization's reputational capital is more important than we previously imagined—more fragile and easily damaged. BP was one obvious example of how technology (in this case, Twitter and YouTube) can wreak havoc on an organization, especially in industries that already face challenges defending their actions.

But in today's information culture, even trusted modern brands such as Amazon, Google, and Starbucks have felt the sting of public revelations they probably would rather have kept within the company. Although each of these brands is regularly cited as exemplary when measured against authenticity criteria such as "a commitment to deliver on its promise," in 2012–2013 all three organizations were brutally and publicly grilled in the UK on their sizable revenues and relatively tiny in-country tax payments. On UK turnover of £207 million in 2011, Amazon paid a mere £1.8 million in tax; in the same year Google recorded UK sales of £2.5 billion and a UK tax charge of just £3.4 million.[10]

The Starbucks story received perhaps the most attention. During thirteen years of trading in the UK, Starbucks generated £3.1 billion in revenues, yet paid just £8.6 million in tax; between 2009 and 2013, it paid zero corporation tax—this, despite chairman and CEO Howard Schultz's oft-cited quote: "Authenticity is what we stand for. It's part of who we are. If we compromise who we are to achieve higher profits, what have we accomplished?" The UK Public Accounts Committee had some choice words of its own for the company. Among other things, the committee found it "difficult to believe" Starbucks's claim that it had been trading at a loss for nearly every year of its UK operations.[11]

The UK committee's investigation of the coffee company attracted significant public interest, broadcast on every possible high-tech venue, as well as on primetime news bulletins and newspaper front pages. In the end, Starbucks—saying that it had heard a message "loud and clear" from its customers—committed to paying £10 million in corporation tax in 2013, and again in 2014—regardless of profit.[12] But the damage had already been done. At least in the UK, Starbucks's reputation had taken a hit.

Human Psychological Needs

As we researched this book, the abiding request we heard from employees and stakeholders was to know one thing: "What's really going on in this organization?" No one likes being left in the dark. Even when the facts are not what people would like to hear, they still want to be treated with the respect that comes with candid communication, rather than having bad news withheld or sugar-coated. There is a human need to know, to be given information to mitigate the sense of powerlessness we feel when we *don't* know what's happening—illustrated by what could be called the "traveler's complaint."

People who travel by rail or air often feel dissatisfied at some point before or during the journey (and sometimes afterward, if luggage is lost!). There are many complaints—late departures, overcrowded conditions, expensive ticket prices, poor food, bad-tempered staff. But always top of the list is the sheer lack of information. If the train is late, passengers want to know why. If the plane is diverted or canceled, travelers would like an explanation. The news may not be good, but at least it's news and it restores one's sense of control over the situation, however illusory that control might actually be.

An extreme and tragic example of this phenomenon occurred in early March 2014 with the disappearance of Malaysia Airlines flight 370 (whose exact whereabouts remain a mystery as of this writing).[13] The passenger flight, which was scheduled to fly from Kuala Lumpur to Beijing, lost contact with air traffic control less than an hour after takeoff. The problem came not just from the fact of the tragedy itself, but also because the relatives of the 239 people aboard the plane were offered little initial information concerning their loved ones' fates. For example, the mandatory report that the airline released to a UN body soon after the disappearance was not made available to the relatives of the passengers. Moreover, a communication breakdown between the airline and air traffic controllers also appears to have delayed the search and rescue effort, according to one report.[14] Amid confusion and misleading information, four hours passed after the last communication from the flight cockpit before a search was activated.

Sadly, a mere four months later, another tragedy struck Malaysian Airlines with the downing over Ukraine of flight 17, en route from Amsterdam to Kuala Lumpur on July 17, 2014. Even with that more recent disaster to contend with, however, the Malaysian government issued a public communication on the airline's website in early August 2014 regarding the March tragedy. Exhibiting an improved awareness of the needs of the lost passengers' relatives, and the human need for continued communication, the statement read: "After five months of searching for the missing plane, we would like to assure the next of kin of MH370 that our commitment to the search for this flight has remained consistent and has strengthened." The announcement went on to say that Australia's Fugro Survey Ltd. had been contracted to conduct an in-depth search of the Indian Ocean floor, where the flight was believed to have been diverted.[15]

Organizational and Regulatory Changes

A third set of forces driving the honesty imperative in organizations today involves the complex structural changes that are making information sharing more and more important. The classic large, international organizations of the twentieth century were held together with hierarchies, organization charts, and job definitions. In such structures, information flows could be relatively easily managed and controlled, with knowledge parceled out "on a need to know basis."

But the more knowledge-based that organizations become, the more they are characterized by multidimensional matrix structures that produce high levels of flexibility and ambiguity—making free-flowing communication systems absolutely imperative.[16] For example, the development of complex pharmaceuticals, the design and manufacture of large commercial aircraft, or the innovation of new mobile communications technology simply cannot proceed within conventional hierarchies. Inevitably, complex structures emerge that aim to facilitate speedier, more flexible reporting relations and easier information flows— without the need to go up and down lengthy hierarchies. Such structures can work only if individuals are given the information and skills they need to respond effectively and continually to diverse organizational challenges. But the major success factor—always—is trust. This is difficult to achieve if information is not shared as openly as possible.

At the same time, increased government regulation in general is driving the need for more honesty and transparency in every kind of organization. Although exacerbated in the financial services sector by the 2008 economic crash, there is a long-standing tradition of government regulation in other areas as well. For example, pharmaceutical companies have long had to live successfully with the likes of the US Food and Drug Administration and the UK's Medicine and Healthcare Products Regulatory Agency. Indeed, the best of these companies put huge efforts into managing their relationships with the regulators openly and honestly.

What Organizations Can Do

So if it's true that people in organizations today require free-flowing communication to do their jobs well, what kinds of information do they need most? The answer to this question clearly connects to arguments that we develop elsewhere in this book in our quest to define our dream organization. First, employees need to know the set of values on which their organization rests. What does it really believe in? We explore this theme in chapter 4 on *authenticity*. Second, employees need to know the purpose of their work—a theme we develop in chapter 5, on *meaning*. Third, they need to know the pattern of constraints that operate on them both organizationally and societally. They crave *simple rules* to govern their activities, which we explore in chapter 6. Apart from those fundamentals, however, there are specific actions that organizations can take. In this section, we offer three organizational imperatives for achieving radical honesty in companies.

Before we look at those recommendations, however, see the sidebar "How Much Are Honesty and Openness Valued in Your Organization?," a diagnostic we used in our research for assessing radical honesty in organizations.

We found that senior executives who took our diagnostic scored strongest on the availability of channels of communication and

Diagnostic: How Much Are Honesty and Openness Valued in Your Organization?

1 = Strongly Disagree   2 = Disagree   3 = Neither Agree Nor Disagree
4 = Agree   5 = Strongly Agree

_____ We are all told the real story.

_____ Information is not manipulated.

_____ It is not disloyal to say something negative.

_____ My manager wants to hear bad news.

_____ Many channels of communication are available to us.

_____ I feel comfortable signing my name to comments I make.

Consider any statement to which you assign a 1 or 2 as worth your sustained attention. An overall score below 18 suggests that this area of your organizational life requires improvement. Ask yourself how long you will give the organization to make genuine progress.

feeling comfortable signing their names to comments. Those in low-discretion roles were less comfortable signing their names or communicating bad news upward. All agreed about the risks of deliberate information distortion: "Information is not manipulated" was the lowest-scoring item in the set.

Significantly, the diagnostic statements point to three areas for action where organizations can make improvements: *make conscious choices around how the company shares information internally;*

develop a culture of openness and trust; and *have a policy of honest information sharing inside and outside the organization.*

Let's look at each of these in turn.

Make Conscious Choices around How the Company Shares Information inside the Organization

This first action step closely corresponds to two statements in the diagnostic, namely, "We are all told the real story" and "Many channels of communication are available to us." This is a call to leaders to remember the importance of keeping the channels of communication open, as well as the need to give careful thought to what, when, and how much information is shared.

Openly communicating with employees was one key to a turnaround that occurred at a US chain of jewelry stores. When Theo Killion took over as CEO of Zales Corp. in 2010, the ninety-year-old company was near bankruptcy, with more than four hundred store closings in the previous years and serious personnel and salary cuts. The new CEO saw that part of his job would be to inspire his dispirited employees—and that free-flowing information would be key. He began by holding "town hall" meetings in the organization to share both good news and bad, and to field questions from all levels of employees. He made personal visits and calls to store managers, and during the holiday season made a point to call and connect with every one of his two hundred regional and district managers. These are practices that Killion continues today and that, along with extreme cost-cutting measures, led to a $10 million year and a tripling in Zales's stock price in 2013—its first profitable year since 2008.[17]

Unfortunately, when communication doesn't happen in organizations, a lot of pain and suffering can result—and it isn't just the private sector that encounters problems. A spate of scandals in Britain around both child care and patient care have highlighted the necessity for open and full information sharing between various state agencies. Police, social workers, and local-authority employees have been roundly condemned in a series of high-profile public inquiries for failing to share information that literally could have saved lives. In one of the most tragic cases involving "Baby P," the victim had been seen by twenty-eight social workers, doctors, and police officers, and had been taken to the hospital nine times before dying after having been intentionally tortured. The subsequent inquiry found that one of the key structural failings was the utter incapability to share information effectively.

That brings us to the topic of *how* information is (or isn't) shared most efficiently and completely. There is a tendency for all of us to obsessively use the channels of communication with which we are most at ease. This is of course wholly understandable. But the modern world is increasingly characterized by multichannel communication. To be effective, individuals must therefore be prepared to leave their comfort zones and master a range of technological modes, including new media, if they hope to communicate across multigenerational workforces and stakeholders.

This is especially true in the kinds of matrix organizations common today, in which complex reporting lines create structures where individuals often report to more than one person. In such organizations the use of influence becomes more important than the exercise of power. Increasing complexity—globalization, rapid innovation cycles, synergistic opportunities, and dissolving boundaries—make matrix structures inevitable. But problems arise because we are placing executives in these organizations who were socialized in a different world, where hoarding information equated to power. It soon becomes clear that one of the key ingredients in successful matrix organizations is high levels of trust, and that a significant builder of trust is open and honest information sharing.

Develop a Culture of Openness and Trust

This second action step is implied (with varying emphasis) in three of the statements from our diagnostic: "It is not disloyal to say something negative," "My manager wants to hear bad news," and "I feel comfortable signing my name to comments I make." The reminder here for leaders is to create an organizational culture in which people feel safe imparting their views.

For example, consider the UK's legendary RAF Red Arrows jet-formation flying team. Their aerobatic maneuvers at breakneck speeds up to six hundred miles an hour are known all over the world. After every display and practice routine they conduct a brutal and public assessment of how each member of the team performed and areas for improvement. Needless to say, this is work where the tiniest of human errors will have catastrophic consequences. There is literally no room for error, and so, in a way, the need to deal with "bad news" is not a choice.

But few workplaces feel quite like this. As a result, there is a need to invent mechanisms to ensure that it is OK to surface problems. The well-known round-the-world sailing competitor, Pete Goss, made a point of establishing what he called "bad news meetings" as a way of ensuring all problems were aired. In another setting Louise Makin, chief executive of BTG—one of the UK's most significant science-based businesses—holds regular meetings that she calls "hopes and fears discussions." Her view is that the key leadership skill is openness: "I need to know bad news, good news, hopes and fears, what might happen, because there is a tendency to think you can't bring the CEO bad news."

An executive vice president we know of, at a privately held US East Coast midsize company, stated the issue this way: "About a third of my people are unskilled workers, and only a few have college degrees. I have a big title, and some people are a bit afraid of that. But my job ultimately is to serve the organization and make it better. I can't do that if people don't come to me when they see problems. So I try to communicate that to my employees." For example, when an employee confronts her about an issue, she tells him or her that she appreciates their candor, and why. And when someone says or does something particularly helpful, she always sends a handwritten note on executive letterhead. "When people know you think they're valuable," she explains, "they feel safer to be open with you in return."

Recall our example of Novo Nordisk, whose company culture in the 1990s implicitly kept bad news from reaching the executive board—and brought the company perilously close to disaster. Since that time, Novo has made serious changes to its communication policies. Now the world's eighth-largest pharmaceutical company and the world's biggest supplier of insulin, Novo has built radical honesty into its method of operations. Using a wide variety of methods to communicate with and listen to stakeholders and employees, the company's commitment to the truth is central. For example, PeopleCom, Novo's internal news module, regularly receives hundreds of vigorous comments from employees about various workings of the company. More remarkable still, employees always opt to have their comments attributed with their full names—which speaks to the trust people have in their employer's core organizational value of openness and honesty.

The extent to which radical honesty is embedded in Novo's culture today is illustrated in an example about the current CEO Lars Reiben Sorensen. When the company decided to close down a research facility in California, Sorensen flew to the facility himself, assembled the workforce, and spoke to them openly about the reasons for the closure and the time scale involved. The astounding response from the employees? Applause.

That anecdote exemplifies, we believe, the promise of radical honesty and what can happen when organizations replace climates of secrecy and suspicion with free-flowing communication.

Have a Policy of Honest Information Sharing, inside and outside the Organization

This final action step is implied in the diagnostic statement, "Information is not manipulated." To be sure, given the unavoidable transparency inherent in today's technological realities, we cannot overstate the importance of being open with all stakeholders and the public.

Novo Nordisk's triple-bottom-line reporting, which we discuss in more detail in the next chapter, illustrates how the content of what a company shares publicly can be radically reconsidered. But beyond this it reminds us of the need to address the differing requirements of distinctive interests and audiences. Increasingly, these go beyond employers and shareholders and certainly include customers, regulatory authorities, and campaign groups. Get this wrong and the consequences can be damaging—as Tesco's miscommunication following the horsemeat scandal showed.

But what kinds of information, exactly, do organizations need to share? With whom? And how? These are no longer questions simply for media businesses—we all now share these concerns. No matter the industry, business, or particular activity, all organizations must manage the media in all its formats, both traditional (print, TV, and radio, for example) and new (web pages, blogs, Twitter feeds). But how is this exponential growth in media channels to be managed?

These are big questions, and we don't claim to have all the answers. Trade secrets, of course, will always require confidentiality. And we don't want to suggest that honesty will necessarily stop problems from arising, particularly in highly regulated industries that routinely find themselves under scrutiny. We maintain, though, that executives should err on the side of radical honesty far more than their instincts suggest. Particularly today, when trust levels among both employees and customers are so low and background noise is so high, organizations must work very hard to communicate what's going on if they are to be heard and believed.

Critical to this discussion is the growing significance of the corporate communications function in organizations. Recent economic history has taught us that reputational capital is becoming both more important and more fragile—think Enron and Arthur Andersen. The problem is that many of the people who populate corporate communications offices have acquired their skills in the world of public relations, press offices, and government liaison posts. They have become habituated to "spin." But in the new world, the imperative is to tell the whole story, warts and all.

So how do we reconcile these apparently contrasting organizational needs? On the one hand there is corporate PR, marketing, and the need to make the organization attractive to potential employees, clients, and investors. On the other hand is a company's responsibility for openness—what we have called radical honesty. Clearly "honesty" cannot be hived off to a separate function. As the trust indices regularly remind us, transparent and honest practices are now seen as the number-one factor in creating corporate reputation. Radical honesty is no longer a luxury; it is a business necessity. Yet at the same time, the achievement of trustworthy transparency involves much more than endless disclosure of often irrelevant and sometimes misleading information.

Consider Heineken's swift and open response to a potential PR nightmare—contrasted with the usual clumsy corporate attempts to divert and deceive that we have seen all too often. The story begins with a posting on Facebook of gruesome images of dog fighting in a nightclub in Mongolia. Banners clearly visible around the nightclub reveal the Heineken® brand, giving the impression that the brand was a sponsor of the event—which was not the case.

The company was taken completely unawares, finding out only when consumers bombarded the Heineken® Facebook page, company website, Twitter account, and customer hotlines with complaints and threats to boycott the brand "for sponsoring dog fighting." Over the next four days, the Heineken corporate website and the brand's Facebook page received more than one hundred thousand visits. This is what the company was aware of; what it did not know was how many of these posts were being shared with friends and friends of friends. And it did not know how this misinformation was affecting the way consumers felt about the brand and what the impact was at point of sale. Were consumers choosing not to buy Heineken® because of this mistaken association with dog fighting? That was a major question.

To tackle the issue, Heineken immediately formed a team to respond to every e-mail, call, or Facebook post to let consumers know it was now aware of the situation. It also stated that Heineken® would never sponsor dog fighting, which the company knew to be a sadistic betting game that positioned the animals in a cruel fight to the death. Heineken assured consumers it would find out what happened and would outline what actions it would take.

Within twenty-four hours, the company's investigations led it to a top nightclub in the capital of Mongolia. The owner had rented his venue to a third party to conduct a private event during the day when the club was not open. The week before, the club had hosted a premium party and had placed Heineken® banners around the bar. Unfortunately, the bar owner did not remove them. So this was why they were visible when the dog fight took place.

Once the company knew what had happened, it immediately severed its relationship with the bar owner in Mongolia, removing all Heineken products. Then it went on the offensive, talking directly to every consumer who had contacted them. Those who appreciated the quick response were asked to share the company position with their friends. The company position paper was put on Heineken.com, heinekeninternational.com, Facebook, and Twitter. The language used was conversational and real. It explained that Heineken® is a brand that supports world-class events like the London 2012 Olympics and Champions League football. What it does not support is dog fighting in Mongolia or anywhere else in the world. The company also reached out to all animal rights groups, explaining what had happened and sharing the position paper and actions taken so that they could respond on its behalf if they received questions.

Within three days the number of positive/neutral posts equaled the number of negative posts. And within a week, more than 90 percent of posts were positive/neutral. Many of those who had been vehemently opposed to the company became supportive because of the way it had responded to the problem.

This was the first time that Heineken® had come under attack through digital channels. But the company got the message loud and clear: consumers now have multiple entry points to the company to share their opinions—opinions that are then shared with tens of thousands of other people all over the globe. By taking the issue seriously, acting quickly, taking actions, communicating directly with all concerned consumers, and doing so in line with its core company value of respect, it was able to minimize the negative impact on the reputation of its flagship brand. In the end, there was no impact whatsoever on sales.

Perhaps most relieved were the company's own employees, who could be proud and reassured by the way Heineken handled the problem. This example shows the clear benefits of honesty, speed of response, and a preparedness to address various stakeholders. But it has to be said that despite its speed, the company was merely acting reactively, rather than proactively. Indeed, as a result of this episode, Heineken has worked to reassess a number of ways in which its ability to handle such scenarios could be improved in the future. For example, the company did not discover the incident on its own; rather, it heard about it first from complaining consumers. Heineken therefore reviewed its approach to online monitoring and implemented a "Mission

Control" program to protect its brand in digital space, ensuring it had key responders in place to address issues that might arise on a variety of communication channels.

———————

At the heart of what we have been arguing in this chapter is the idea that radical honesty is an increasingly important critical success factor for organizations. But we have also been arguing that honesty both within organizations and between organizations and the wider society arises from social relationships in which trust plays a major part. To put this more philosophically, trust is not something that can be specified in a contract—it has a much more diffuse quality. In the next chapter, we turn our attention to the ways in which authentic organizations make it their mission to add value to their people, rather than merely extracting value from them.

Action Points for Leaders

✔ **Communicate honestly and quickly.** You have less time than you think. Modern technologies have dramatically speeded the dissemination of information. Make sure, however, you are focused on what's most important to tell people. Radical honesty is proactive.

✔ **Use many communications channels.** Remember, you are attempting to reach individuals and groups within and beyond your organization with different communicative habits. There may be marked generational variations. Younger people will use social media, older generations may rely on face-to-face contact and networks. Recognize your default mode and experiment with other channels.

✔ **Encourage radically honest conversations about people's hopes and fears throughout the organization.** Power relationships tend to sanitize the information that reaches the top. You will need to find a way of knowing what's really going on. Take a deep dive into your organization, collecting information that hasn't yet been sanitized. Allow people to bring you bad news—make it feel safe for them. Radical honesty works both ways.

✔ **Keep communication as simple as possible.** There is a need for more trustworthy and relevant information that can be comprehended—not more and more data and details that cannot. Some organizations confuse sharing data with effective communication. This is a mistake. Who reads the myriad conditions that apply to their credit cards?

✔ **Build in feedback loops.** Remember that trust builds slowly but can be destroyed in an instant. Provide multiple opportunities for stakeholders to communicate back. This can range from "old-fashioned" techniques such as management by walking around (MBWA) to more contemporary use of social media.

Chapter 3

Build on People's Strengths and Interests

*Creating Extra Value
for Everyone*

The need for organizations to develop their human capital will not come as big news to anyone. It has long been recognized by elite knowledge-intensive businesses like Goldman Sachs, McKinsey, and Johns Hopkins Hospital. More recent examples include Microsoft, Google, and Apple. But we contend that this process is not confined to specialized, high-tech, or high-finance organizations or occupations. It will increasingly become characteristic of the wider employment relationship, including in traditional "blue-collar" industries and franchises such as McDonald's, whose UK training program in hospitality and catering awards employees with nationally recognized academic qualifications.

The fact is, the challenge of finding, training, and retaining excellent workers has always been with us. But meeting that challenge today requires a seismic shift in the employee-employer relationship. In the authentic organization, rather than ceaselessly extracting value from employees, "extra" value is *added* (signified by the "E" in our DREAMS organization). The ideal company doesn't just grow its best employees; it makes all its employees better than they ever thought they could be. Rather than thinking about how much they can get out of every person, these organizations think about how much they can magnify their strengths. At heart, that's what productivity improvement really means. High-productivity organizations are typically distinguished by continuous investment in their people.

This is an apparently simple idea and yet it is surprising that in the second decade of the twenty-first century, so few organizations have fully embraced its implications. At the most basic level of why adding value matters to organizations and individuals, there is a mountain of studies linking investment in the various types of human capital with job satisfaction, productivity, greater retention, lower turnover, and other benefits. This in turn is linked with customer retention and satisfaction.[1] Interestingly, the link with performance is often explained in terms of inducing employee discretionary behavior.[2] This means that magnifying employees' strengths results in workers who do more, better, and more innovatively. Linking all of this causally to financial performance (e.g., profitability or shareholder value) is more difficult, mainly because of time-lag effects and intervening variables. But over the long term, there is a correlation between financial performance and investment in human capital.[3]

In this chapter, we address several questions: What does value mean, and how is it added? What forms does it take, and how is it developed? Within each of these questions we will also look at who in the organization is responsible for making sure employees receive added value. And as we have done in the previous two chapters, we will also introduce a diagnostic and explore the organizational and leadership imperatives that follow from the diagnostic statements.

Let's begin with a look at where the idea of value adding came from in the first place.

Valuing Value

The idea of "value" as it relates to the purpose and management of employees has changed radically over time. Indeed, as mercantile capitalism emerged from feudalism, one of the key debates about how society and organizations should be run was ultimately concerned with the concept of value and how value is created. As modern social science developed a little later, the concept of value was central to the exchanges between Adam Smith and David Ricardo. Then in the nineteenth century, as Marx sought to develop a critique of political economy, both Smith's and Ricardo's theories of value were among those ideas with which he actively engaged. Accordingly, Marxist theories became one of two competing theories—the other is neoclassical economics—that have dominated the modern history of the capitalist enterprise. Neoclassical economics explains the origins of profit as a payment for the exercise of entrepreneurship. According to the logic of this theory, a company's founders and, later, shareholders, receive profit as a reward for the risk they take by investing.

The managerial analogue to neoclassical economics—Taylorism—dominated theories of management in the early twentieth century. Based on the work of Frederick Winslow Taylor, the "father" of scientific management and the efficiency movement, Taylorism rests on the radical separation of the labor of conception (thinking) and the labor of execution (doing).[4] Thinking is concentrated in the hands of management and doing in the hands of the worker. The task of managers is to get workers to do more.

Marxist theories, on the other hand, explain profit as arising from the extraction of value from employees who receive in wages less than the full value of what they create. Marxist approaches therefore proposed the theory of worker alienation—where employees suffer as a result of separation both from the product of their labor and from the act of labor itself as work is transformed from a creative act into an instrumental one. Workers sell their time, and it is the task of the capitalist to ensure that the time is used productively. The complex dance that ensues is wonderfully captured in the later work of the US industrial anthropologist Donald Roy, writing in the late 1940s and early 1950s.[5] His participant observational studies of machine shop operatives in Chicago show how workers pour their creativity into cheating the piece-work system—ensuring that on jobs where they cannot make a bonus, they limit effort, only throwing themselves into their work when they have found a way of guaranteeing maximum piece-work returns (the workers call this distinction the difference between "stinkers" and "gravy jobs").

Both Marxist and neoclassical economic theories have drawbacks, and according to recent data on engagement in the workplace, the problems generated by both Taylorism and Marxism have never been resolved. Neoclassical economics has been undermined by the growth of the managerial class, presciently described in Berle and Means's *The Managerial Revolution*.[6] The authors contend that the modern giant capitalist enterprise is responsible not to its shareholders but to its management. Recent scandals rather support this view. The ramifications of the Enron debacle continue to ripple. The view that the capitalist enterprise is unequivocally responsible to its shareholders has been severely damaged. The financial crash of 2008 has done little to restore faith in current patterns of corporate governance. The neoclassical theory is further undermined by the changing nature of shareholders. Shares are increasingly held not as a form of long-term investment by those who have a stake in the success of the organization, but as a commodity in their own right to be traded ever more quickly. In fact, the average length of share ownership is now a mere twenty-two seconds.[7] The recent scandal of the "dark pools," where high-intensity traders have shared space with big institutional investors, has further complicated the picture. This is explored in Michael Lewis's book *Flash Boys*, which examines the role of high-intensity trading on the stock market.[8]

Likewise, the Marxian argument has been challenged by the persistent observation that the most successful capitalist companies are characterized by investing in their employees—adding value, not extracting it. In other words, Marx conceived of the struggle over value to be a zero-sum game, in which whatever the capitalist gained would be a loss for the worker. Yet modern organizations show this to be clearly false—capitalists and workers both do better by concentrating on how value gets added all around. But the way this plays out in organizations may reflect conflicting ideas about value creation. At the beginning of this chapter we mentioned McDonald's training and development efforts. But the precise specification and discipline of its work routines reflect the continuing influence of Taylorist ideas. As we write this in 2014, in Chicago two thousand workers are on the streets with placards reading: "No Big Macs, no fries, make our wages supersize!" Employees are protesting the minimum wage paid by the restaurant chain to its frontline staff—while the CEO has a proposed pay package of $9.5 million.[9]

Curiously, Taylorism and Marxism have much in common (perhaps this explains why Lenin was such an admirer of F. W. Taylor). They both see the workplace as fundamentally contested terrain. For Marx, the struggle is between workers and capitalists. For Taylor, it is between managers and recalcitrant employees. But the assumptions on which both these paradigms rest no longer give us a handle on the modern company. Perhaps it is time that the thinking of both Henry Ford—another advocate of Taylorism—and Lenin are consigned to the "dustbin of history."

What Is Value, and How Is It Added?

Just what are we talking about when we talk about value? Consider the following examples.

- A UK teenager from a Vietnamese family with few formal qualifications decides to leave school to help support her family. She is offered a job at McDonald's, and within months not only can she can make a cheeseburger, but she also understands the pricing system for various packaged meals, and is beginning to think about working toward becoming a team shift leader.

- A PhD scientist from Roche pharmaceuticals works in a disease area that requires her to understand and observe soft tissue in the body. Roche teaches her how to use a new and complex MRI scanner to do the job, and also promotes her to team leader, which will challenge her interpersonal skills. Her responsibilities have suddenly become much wider.

- A young assistant professor at an elite US business school is sponsored to attend the Academy of Management conference in Europe. He has just finished the paper he is presenting and is keen to make sure he interacts with his colleagues in Europe who specialize in the same field. His long-term plan is to set up a network of researchers who can cooperate on his next project.

- A new college graduate in South Africa who was at the top of her class is recruited by J. Walter Thompson, the global marketing communications firm. She is exposed to the full range of marketing skills, and to her considerable delight works on a project with colleagues in New York. The work is great, but better still, she soon sees that having experience at JWT may bring other opportunities her way—she quickly finds herself on the radar screen of employment agencies and other search consultants.

- A twenty-year-old, living in Madrid, has been unemployed since leaving high school and is experiencing an increasing sense of loneliness and hopelessness. Out of the blue he gets the chance to join the mail room at a major telecoms company. Within months he feels part of a team who make a difference to the efficiency of the organization. He is starting at the bottom of the company, but nevertheless his sense of self begins to move in the right direction.

These vignettes tell us a lot about different kinds of value that can be added. We can think of each type of value as representing one of three categories of skills: technical, conceptual, or human.[10]

Technical skills are typically understood as job-specific knowledge and techniques that individuals require to fulfill their work tasks. Much of this learning takes place on the job and is the responsibility of line executives, though this process may be accelerated by short, intensive training courses. Technical skills are often a major focus for the development of lower-level employees who need to understand various tools and techniques to produce the organization's products and services. So they are important, for example, to the Vietnamese teenager working for McDonald's. But technical skills are important also for the scientist at Roche, the US business professor, and the young marketer in South Africa. They will all have developed technical skills, and some of these go beyond occupationally specific competencies. So the Roche scientist will be learning how to use the very latest medical equipment, and the training may be delivered by the supplier of the machinery, like GE Medical, Siemens, or Philips. Or think of the highly quantitative trader in an investment bank who will receive intensive training in the latest techniques of algorithmic analysis. The paradox here is that technical skills begin to run out hierarchically. It is inconceivable that the head of R&D at Novartis or Pfizer is the best scientist in the company. As the R&D head moves through the hierarchy, her task becomes to employ and develop people who are technically better than she is.

Conceptual skills typically become important in more senior occupations where there is a need to understand the organization as a whole, the relationships among its parts, and how it connects with its broader environment. These skills are often developed by sending executives to business schools, where they are exposed to the latest thinking on strategy and organizational behavior. For example, conceptual skills will likely become more important for the Roche scientist as she takes on her team leadership role. She will need to become aware of the rapidly changing science base that has characterized pharmaceutical companies for years—for example, the move from chemistry to biochemistry and genetics. Even more difficult, she will have to learn about the complexities of managing and leading in the kinds of matrix structures we described in the last chapter, which are increasingly characteristic of R&D departments and other complex task environments. Or think about the marketer in a fast-moving consumer goods company like Unilever, Nestle, or Procter & Gamble—he or she must come to terms with the new reality of social and digital media, essentially rethinking his or her view of the world. This is a paradigmatically conceptual competence.

Human skills, like conceptual skills, traditionally have been seen as increasingly important as a person takes on more managerial responsibilities—which require the individual, in one way or another, to deliver performance through other people. The truth is rather more complex. Our experience of "clever" MBA students in some organizations with which we've worked is that they often massively exaggerate the importance of technical and conceptual skills—and miss entirely the vital need for human competencies. It can come as a nasty shock indeed, ten years following graduation, to discover that high performance is rarely achieved without the cooperation of others.

Many organizations start to become concerned with developing human skills only once an employee has taken on a managerial or leadership position. At that point, HR will develop and provide interpersonal-skills programs, and high-potential executives will be increasingly exposed to the top leadership in the hope (often vain) that they will be influenced by the exemplary conduct of their senior leaders. Very smart organizations, however, recognize the significance of human skills *throughout* the hierarchy—for example, the skill of the bartender who makes eye contact with customers, or the skill of the receptionist at a hotel or bank who makes customers feel significant.

The fact is that human skills are required in each of the examples we described earlier, from the Roche pharmaceuticals scientist to the young US business professor and the Vietnamese teenager. In simple terms, organizations can add value to employees through a varying mix of technical, human, and conceptual skills. This conceptual framework is extremely useful but the more recent obsession of "human capital theory" invites us to develop a more complex picture, starting with the very concept of "skill."[11] There is clearly a difference between learning to cook a cheeseburger and understanding the output of a sophisticated MRI scanner. In addition, some skills are extremely hard to codify. The creative executive at a music company can't really tell you why he decides to sign one band rather than another. But if he gets it right, he becomes a very valuable employee indeed.

Within the "human skills" category, an important source of value lies in the building of both internal and external networks. The Roche scientist struggling to lead her team within the matrix structure will need a very well-developed internal network. But like the US professor, she also needs a strong external network of like-minded scientists. For example, we recently had the opportunity to sit in an audience of mostly R&D folks at another innovative pharmaceutical company. When we asked the people on either side of us, "What's your job?" they speedily answered, "I'm a scientist." It became clear that these professionals' sense of self arose from their occupation—not from their organization. It also was clear that their network of fellow scientists stretched way beyond the boundaries of their organization.

We were reminded of the old sociological distinction between occupational and organizational communities. Some derive their identity not so much from their occupation, but more from the organization that employs them (e.g., "I'm an IBMer"). Typically, the "old" professions like lawyer or doctor give rise to occupational identity. But some of the modern giant corporations like Google, Apple, and Microsoft have such strong cultures that identity becomes increasingly organizational. One longtime Apple executive told us, "We work fourteen hours a day, we party ten hours a day, and we sleep the rest!" And of course, they partied with other Apple executives.

When it comes to an external network, clearly the young South African marketer is gaining value by being associated with such a prestigious firm as JWT. To be sure, as we saw in the last chapter on radical honesty, reputational capital is simultaneously more important and more fragile than we previously imagined. Arthur Andersen, for example, went from being arguably the greatest professional services firm in the world to not existing in about a month, because somebody shredded documents. Goldman Sachs's carefully nurtured elite brand was damaged by Greg Smith's excoriating resignation letter accusing the company of not living up to its own standards.

Despite this fragility, we live in a world where reputational (and network) capital often becomes more important than the simple acquisition of technical skill. For example, the MBA curricula of most business schools around the world are more or less identical, and as a generalist degree, the depth of knowledge within each subject discipline is far less than with a specialist qualification. So content and delivery vary little. Why then do individuals pay a significant premium to attend the elite schools? The answer clearly lies with the acquisition of a valuable, lifelong network and the blessing of a prestigious brand. The top schools recruit the best students, thus creating a virtuous circle. As they graduate, they have a vested interest in maintaining the power of the brand. Similarly, no one ever got fired for hiring IBM or a consulting team from McKinsey to work with their company.

When we consider the topic of networks more broadly, we find the notion of "cultural capital" becomes applicable. This idea is most clearly expressed in the work of sociologist Pierre Bordieu, who argues that just as social groups in society have differential access to material resources, so is access to the most desired cultural forms limited.[12] In literature, art, TV, fashion, and food, elite social groups are able to make their definition of culture the most "desirable." In organizations, the phenomenon emerges in the form of cultural barriers that make it hard for people to move through the hierarchy. Barriers regarding gender, for example, are often referred to as the "glass ceiling," but cultural exclusion in organizations encompasses many subtle forms—class, educational background, region, accent—all of which may inhibit upward social mobility and other forms of extra value that the organization might add to employees' lives.

Social or organizational groups may even create a complex cultural screening program to exclude others from elite positions. For example, perhaps we are now seeing the creation of a new elite among the tech gurus of Silicon Valley. Some people have already started to call it i-apartheid, as an increasingly narrow rather than diverse population—white, male, well-educated—in the Valley has produced its own kind of separated and introverted conformity. The signs are certainly worrying. Here is one description of this new elite's encroachment:

Every morning and every evening the fleet glides through the city, hundreds of white buses with tinted windows navigating San Francisco's rush hour. From the pavement you can see your reflection in the windows, but you can't see in. The buses have no markings or logos, no advertised destinations or stops.

It doesn't matter. Everyone knows what they are. "Transport for a breed apart. For a community that is separate but not equal," said Diamond Dave Whitaker, a self-professed beat poet and rabble-rouser.[13]

The *San Francisco Chronicle* recently swelled the chorus with an op-ed denouncing the private shuttles as symbols of alienation and division: "San Franciscans feel resentful about the technology industry's lack of civic and community engagement, and the Google bus is our daily reminder."[14]

But even those who feel most excluded from the environment comprising their daily lives or their organizations may still gain value through what might be called the socializing effects of work. Employment can be a route to self-esteem and physical and mental well-being, as our twenty-year-old in Madrid illustrates. Conversely, experience from the Great Depression of the 1930s shows that exclusion from work has long-term deleterious effects. And today, the high levels of youth unemployment, characteristic of many parts of the Western world, suggest we may be sitting on a mental health time bomb. So the value added by even the most basic internal workplace network appears to be great indeed.

Whether value is being added with human skills, technical skills, or conceptual skills, or a bit of all of these, what becomes immediately clear is that the organizational processes and leadership activities that support adding value have a rhythm and time scale of their own. Some are fast, like the acquisition of a basic technical skill; some are long-term, like the building of networks.

Some are tangible and need to be measured; some are less tangible and can only be felt tacitly by the employee herself. And some are easily transferable; others are not.

Likewise, the responsibility for ensuring that value is added to the human capital in organizations will vary from case to case. In the following section we will learn more about how this gets done.

What Organizations Can Do

Now that we've explored some of the various forms of added value, let's look at the ways organizations can begin to add value in practice. Note that because in elite knowledge-intensive organizations, the responsibility for development rests mainly with individuals themselves, employees have to be quite proactive in seeking out the knowledge they need and the networks to support them. In the case of LOCOG and McDonald's, by contrast, we can see strategic HR at its very best. In both examples the human resource function is at the heart of adding value, and in both cases its success is measured with elaborate and strict metrics. Interestingly, the HR functions of both organizations exhibit that combination of leading-edge people practices and considerable business "savvy," which may be the key ingredients of really successful strategic HR.

Before we look at specific methods for adding value, check out the sidebar "Does Your Organization Magnify Your Strengths?" It contains a portion of the diagnostic we use in our work with organizations to help us identify "dream" companies—those that understand what it means to add value *to* the people who work for them, not just taking all the value they can *from* those employees.

In our surveys, senior executives—perhaps not surprisingly— feel most strongly that they are given the chance to develop and are least convinced that the weakest performers can see ways to

Diagnostic: Does Your Organization Magnify Your Strengths?

1 = Strongly Disagree   2 = Disagree   3 = Neither Agree Nor Disagree
4 = Agree   5 = Strongly Agree

_____ I am given the chance to develop.

_____ Every employee is given the chance to develop.

_____ The best people want to perform here.

_____ The weakest performers can see a path to improvement.

_____ Compensation is fairly distributed throughout the organization.

_____ We generate value for ourselves by adding value to others.

Consider any statement to which you assign a 1 or 2 as worth your sustained attention. An overall score below 18 suggests that this area of your organizational life requires improvement. Ask yourself how long you will give the organization to make genuine progress.

---

improve. Among other employees the strongest-scoring item is "We generate value for ourselves by adding value to others." As we will discuss elsewhere (chapter 5), this might be explained by the opportunities that are available—even to those in relatively routine operative or service occupations—to exceed role expectations and deliver extra value to consumers or customers.

Note that each of the diagnostic statements implies an important organizational and leadership imperative. In fact, our research uncovered three primary ways that companies can add extra value and magnify their people's strengths: through opportunities for personal and professional development, by helping stars to shine and weak players to grow, and by leveraging the dynamic inherent in the act of adding value. Let's look at each of these methods.

Offer Opportunities for Development

This imperative corresponds to the diagnostic statements "I am given the chance to develop" and "Every employee is given the chance to develop." These two statements, apparently similar, point to an important difference. The first refers to organizations where particular individuals, such as high potentials or fast trackers, may be developed. The second refers to organizations with a generalized commitment to the development of all: to make the best people the best they can be, and the mediocre performers better than they ever dreamed. As we've already mentioned, knowledge-based companies have been familiar with the terrain of adding value for many years, and they understand the significance to employees of things like reputation, networks, and even cultural capital.

For example, the consulting firm McKinsey, which recruits bright young people from elite business schools all over the world, from the very start is in the business of adding value to its people. Clearly and most obviously, the firm develops conceptual skills, vital for a strategic consulting practice. But much more subtly, over time it provides employees with elaborate networks and significant reputational capital. When people choose to leave McKinsey, they often become chief executives of *Fortune* 500 companies, and the familiar story is that when you leave McKinsey, you become its next client.

Yet as we also suggested earlier, the issue of adding value is not restricted to such knowledge-intensive businesses. It also can be about adding value to the marginal and alienated. To get a sense of how far employee development can be taken, consider the volunteer training effort undertaken by the London Organising Committee of the Olympic Games and Paralympic Games (LOCOG). LOCOG was responsible for mobilizing the largest peacetime workforce ever assembled in the UK, coordinating more than 110,000 subcontractors, 8,500 paid staff, and a massive volunteer group. With numbers reaching 70,000, the volunteer group stands out as a model because of the variety of imaginative methods LOCOG used to employ and manage people of all ages, genders, and ethnicities—many of whom had never worked or volunteered before.

Despite the large number of volunteers, LOCOG was quite deliberately set up as a business. Its chief executive, Paul Deighton, was a former Goldman Sachs investment banker. LOCOG applied rigorous business disciplines to all that it did, and it delivered both on budget and on time. Its successful initiatives included the Trailblazer Volunteer program, in which paid staff learned how to work effectively with volunteers of all social backgrounds. Another program, called Personal Best (initiated by the government and run through a partnership with other state agencies), enabled long-term-unemployed individuals, some with physical or learning disabilities, to earn a job qualification through volunteering. Personal Best also dispatched tutors to help volunteers secure further learning and employment opportunities.

More than 7,500 people enrolled in Personal Best, and the initiative facilitated more than 58,000 volunteering hours. A full 40 percent of participants came from black and minority ethnic communities; 22 percent had a long-term disability, health problem, or learning difficulty. Yet some 20 percent of the Personal Best graduates found employment or went into further training or education after the Olympic and Paralympic Games were over. Building on that success, the Personal Best program is now available in fifty-four centers in England.

Yet another LOCOG initiative, the School Leaver program, targeted students who had left school in East London (where the host borough for the games was located) and other parts of the UK by granting them two 3-month placements in different areas of the organization that, upon completion, were followed by a contract for employment until the end of the Olympic and Paralympic events. Participants included a teenager of Afro-Caribbean descent, Rheiss Brown, who ended up working for LOCOG for a full five years. At first he was hesitant to join the organization. "I assumed that it would be a place where you had to change yourself to fit in," he remembers, "but when I first visited that was so far from the truth. It's the best thing that happened to me. I gained twenty-five years' experience in five."

In the end, LOCOG's influence extended far beyond delivery of the Olympic and Paralympic Games in 2012. By working in partnership with UK government agencies and private-sector employment bureaus, the committee was able to rewrite its work-engagement guidelines to tap into and foster the skill sets in a wider range of people than had previously been considered employable.

Give Weaker Performers a Path to Improvement

For too long HR departments have been obsessed with high-potential employees (sometimes referred to in HR circles as "HiPos"), instead of adding value right across the range of the workforce. But the workplace of our dreams doesn't offer special development just to its stars. Rather, it understands the benefits of adding value to the "average" employee—as reflected by our diagnostic statements "The best people want to perform here" and "The weakest performers can see a path to improvement."

Consider the case of Kind Healthy Snacks' CEO Daniel Lubetzky, who has strong opinions about letting people go: "There are corporate environments where a person has dedicated their life to working hard, and then they're fired with a security person escorting them out the door. I find that so demeaning and disrespectful." While he acknowledges that in the case of intentional dishonesty, a dramatic response might be warranted, "The vast majority of people who work have the best intentions." Unfortunately, sometimes an employee simply doesn't fit with the job at hand. When such a situation arises at Kind Healthy Snacks, Lubetzky takes very specific steps to help the employee improve. Apart from maintaining close and consistent communication and offering regular feedback, Lubetzky works with the person to create a thirty- or sixty-day plan, depending on the situation, for developing the skills needed for improvement. In the end, both the company and the employee win.[15]

How else might organizations add value to their weaker performers? A major global bank we worked with recently is full of people who have considerable technical expertise but lack the high-level human competences that you might find in, for example, a fast-moving consumer goods company. Our intervention has been to stimulate an interest in leadership and a demand for further leadership training. We began with the top team and sought feedback from their colleagues. Very quickly we were able to dive deep into front-line areas of operation where extremely competent technical specialists were hungry for personal development that could improve both their own and their teams' performance. We've been amazed by the response. For some, it's like a light going on in their heads—and suddenly, rather late in their careers, they develop the insatiable demand for leadership skills development. The shift in attitude is already having a positive impact on the bank's performance.

Or consider the example of British food retailer Waitrose after it recently acquired a large supermarket site from a competitor. The acquired store had been characterized by lethargic service, sloppy systems, and an inadequate customer experience. Waitrose made a promise, however, to invest in developing all the existing staff it inherited—a promise in keeping with a critical element of Waitrose culture, as a catalyst for individual change. The impact of the company's deep and passionate commitment to the continuous development of all employees (or partners, as Waitrose calls them) has been dramatic for the newly acquired supermarket. The store is performing so well that it has even driven up local property prices. The major problem Waitrose is left with is the parking lot: usually half empty under the previous ownership, it is too small for the level of demand now created.

Leverage the Dynamic Hidden in Adding Value

This organizational imperative corresponds to the statements in the diagnostic, "We generate value for ourselves by adding value to others" and "Compensation is fairly distributed throughout the organization." Note that the first statement works on both an organizational level and an individual level, in which any value added (to oneself or to an organization) fosters a positive virtuous cycle of continued and expanded value adding. Companies need to recognize that *adding* value to employees and *generating* value as an organization are not competing activities. They are clearly symbiotic: add value to make value. In addition, the distribution of rewards needs to be perceived as broadly fair. In fact, income inequalities at work have risen dramatically in most of the Western world.

Zhang Ruimin, CEO of the highly successful Chinese company Haier, picks up on the value-adding theme as follows:

> I want each employee coming to work for Haier to have the sense that he or she can find a place in the company to realize his or her own values as well as creating value for the enterprise. I have no desire to oversupervise employees. Nor is my goal to grow the company to a certain size. The list of the world's largest 500 companies changes dramatically every decade. Size is no protection against failure if you are not able to fill each employee with vitality. Instead, I want Haier to get to the point where all employees create their own value on a globalized platform. If we are able to accomplish this, we can make Haier a very competitive enterprise.[16]

More prosaically, think of your favorite bar or restaurant. What makes it your favorite? Most likely it's the food, the service, and the ambience, yet all of those things also rest on the skill of the staff. Value added in one area generates increased value in another, and another, and another. This point relates to the opening of this chapter, where we argued that both Taylorist and Marxian accounts of the workplace are flawed. Neither theory grasps the idea that adding value enriches both employers and employees—and of course delights customers. This is not to say, however, that there are not still legitimate questions about how the value created is distributed.

McDonald's offers a view of the value-added dynamic in practice with its two-semester, blended learning curriculum that culminates with a five-day capstone simulation at the company's own Hamburger University, where general managers learn how to develop department managers and to create and execute business plans.

The virtuous cycle triggered when employees become better educated cannot be overstated. Knowledge begets more knowledge—and knowledge sharing. One can imagine how a frontline of qualified workers sharing their latest learnings with their shift teams changes the whole working environment for the better. Customers on the other side of the counter also will experience those improvements in product and service when ordering their burger and fries. And of course the dynamic reverberates further out to the franchise owners and to corporate headquarters, where lowered employee turnover rates (satisfied workers don't tend to leave their jobs) mean money saved in hiring and training costs.

Consider another example, a well-known, prestigious luxury goods company with which we worked, where a key value-add for employees is reputational capital. Part of the company culture is to recruit "well-developed" people—that is, individuals who have received extensive management and leadership development—

from companies such as L'Oreal, Unilever, and Procter & Gamble, and then see how they can adapt to the considerable opportunities they are given. In this highly entrepreneurial firm, "employee development" takes a different form. If the new recruits can thrive (or even simply survive) in this competitive environment, they acquire considerable value in the labor market after leaving the company. The tricky question for them can be when to cash in this value. This is a key consideration for both employees and executives in this organization. At what point in a person's career is the value added crystallized? At the big four accounting firms, for instance, there is always a raft of people who at some point realize they won't make it to partner. Some have left it too late and must come to terms with becoming "career directors"—not always happily.

Yet another way that organizations can leverage the dynamic of value adding is by thinking differently about the larger world of relationships outside the firm—with clients, customers, communities, and wider stakeholders. Organizations need to find ways to build these partners into their consultation and decision processes such that value is added all around. For one of the best examples we've found, see the sidebar, "Novo Nordisk Asks: Are We Financially, Socially, and Environmentally Responsible?"

Another powerful example comes from EY's UK office, which created an initiative that offers staff the opportunity to make a social contribution in their communities while growing their skills and contributing to their careers. For example, one charity set up by EY with the Private Equity Foundation, called ThinkForward, pairs EY employees with marginalized community members through mentoring that helps young people to build more positive futures by making the bridge between school and work, thereby reducing their risk of joining the NEETs (young people who are "Not in employment, education or training"). EY's and other similar corporate initiatives have received positive responses from younger partners in the firm and are seen as a way in which EY can deliberately differentiate itself in the labor market.

Novo Nordisk Asks: Are We Financially, Socially, and Environmentally Responsible?

"We believe that a healthy economy, environment and society are fundamental to long-term business success. This is why we manage our business in accordance with the Triple Bottom Line (TBL) business principle and pursue business solutions that maximize value to our stakeholders as well as our shareholders.

"In practice, this means that any decision should always seek to combine three considerations: is it financially, socially and environmentally responsible? This way, we continuously optimise our business performance and enhance our contribution to the societies we operate in.

"The Triple Bottom Line business principle is anchored in the Novo Nordisk Way and in our Articles of Association (bylaws) that state that Novo Nordisk 'strives to conduct its activities in a financially, environmentally and socially responsible way.'[a]

The Triple Bottom Line maximizes value. ". . . Doing business in a responsible and sustainable way, with a focus on improving public health, benefits patients, society and shareholders. By providing better treatment, raising awareness and advocating for earlier diagnosis and improved health outcomes, we enable people with chronic conditions to live healthier, longer and more productive lives. By promoting responsible and ethical business practices throughout our global value chain and continuously reducing the negative environmental impacts generated by our activities, we stimulate economic growth that is socially just and environmentally sustainable. Finally, TBL makes good business. It delivers long-term growth for our business by building trust, protecting and enhancing our licence to operate and attracting and retaining the best people."

a. The Novo Nordisk Way is a publication that broadly states the company values and is rooted in company origins while providing a guide to the future.

Source: "Our Triple Bottom Line," Novo Nordisk, http://www.novonordisk. com/sustainability/how-we-manage/the-triple-bottom-line.html.

It is also worth noting that the government has a role in adding value to businesses and organizations. It creates an infrastructure framework that allows organizations to thrive. Part of this has to do with things like education, transport, and health, but it also involves creating a legal and regulatory framework that encourages innovation and entrepreneurship. For example, innovation in the pharmaceutical industry is absolutely dependent on a bedrock of intellectual property law. Contemporary political debate often centers on the proper extent of government regulatory controls. In chapter 7 we address this issue more fully.

Another example of leveraging external stakeholders to bring extra value to employees' lives is the House of St Barnabas (HoSB), the London nonprofit members-only social club that we introduced in chapter 1. Partnering with the catering company Benugo has helped it fulfill its mission to provide sustained employment for the homeless, and surplus from the club's membership fees and revenues funds its Employment Academy for homeless participants and its charitable programs. When they began the project in 2013, HoSB chairman David Evans and CEO Sandra Schembri thought they'd see mostly problems directly associated with homelessness, such as addictions. But instead they found that "the heart of the issue is lack of self-esteem," according to Evans. "The academy provides technical and team skills of course . . . but more than that it is trying to change people who don't trust the institution of work. To teach them that work is a two-way street. That there are opportunities—but that this requires networks—social capital."

Schembri adds: "It's about showing people opportunity"—including a cultural program with concerts and other kinds of performances that is "open to members and those that work here, as well as the public. This is another way in which we are adding value to people who often have no such experiences previously." The academy runs a twelve-week employment preparation program several times per year with twenty-five or so people attending each. The aim is to enable participants to be "job ready" for work in the hospitality sector. Talk about a virtuous cycle of adding value! The program is supported by a mentoring network. A few get offered permanent jobs in the club itself; others seek employment in the many local Soho restaurants and hotels—some of whom are partnering with HoSB. To date, HoSB has already generated 550 potential employer opportunities for its participants.

We recognize that when organizations promise to bring out the best in their people, they are entering into a high-risk, high-reward strategy. It raises reputational capital, and such capital is easily destroyed. Once a company heads down this road, it has to commit to keep going—or suffer accordingly. At the very least, a value-adding strategy implies that we must begin to think differently about relationships with employees, customers, and communities. This is a theme that we continue in the next chapter, as we discuss the significance of authenticity in the ideal organization.

Action Points for Leaders

✔ **Offer opportunities for adding extra value in people's personal development as well as professional development.** Conceptualize extra value in rich and diverse ways—think about all of the various forms of value that we have described. This is about much more than the simple development of technical skills and the deployment of training budgets. Remember that some forms of value may be developed speedily while others are slow burn.

✔ **Recognize that adding value to employees and generating value as an organization are not competing activities.** They are clearly symbiotic. Add value to make value. Great pharma companies recruit talented scientists who are obsessed with their scientific expertise, but to this they add critical leadership abilities that drive successful drug development. Or think of your favorite bar or restaurant: the food, the service, and the ambiance all add value—and all of them rest on the skill of the staff.

✔ **Help your star employees to shine and your weaker players to grow.** Don't restrict development to your best workers. Understand that there are considerable benefits from adding value to the "average" employee. For too long HR departments have been obsessed with high-potential employees (HiPos); think instead of adding value right across the range.

✔ **Think in terms of adding extra value in your relationships with clients, customers, and wider stakeholders.** Build them into your consultation and decision processes to create and strengthen a continuous, virtuous cycle of adding value.

✔ **Use outside opportunities for your organization to add value to individuals.** The creative use of temporary assignments and sabbaticals can have a tremendous effect in creating extra value for people. These placements can be with customers or suppliers. More boldly, organizations such as PwC have been moving people to charities in developing countries. The purpose is to supply rich and different experiences that challenge assumptions and drive development.

Chapter 4

Stand for Something Real

Putting Authenticity at the Core

Organizational mission statements are famous for their meaningless verbosity, a fact on which the hugely popular website Dilbert's Automatic Mission Statement Generator capitalized for a while (sadly, it was taken down a few years ago, much to the chagrin of its fans). Consider, for example, the following two mission statements:

> "To continually foster world-class infrastructures as well as to quickly create principle-centered sources to meet our customer's needs."

> "Respect, integrity, communication and excellence." [1]

While the first statement lends new meaning to the word *ambiguous*—and it is, in fact, the product of the Dilbert generator—no doubt we've all seen statements similarly oblique. The second mission statement, however, is mercifully clear. The problem is it came from Enron. Even clear and simple statements run a terrible risk of being inauthentic.

So did we learn the lessons of Enron? Apparently not. WorldCom, Tyco, Parmalat, Northern Rock, VW, Siemens, Deutsche Post, and a host of global banks have all in recent times shocked us with tales of corporate corruption. It is hardly surprising that people are deeply skeptical about business organizations. Each edition of the *Wall Street Journal* and the *Financial Times* brings yet more evidence of the lack of integrity at the core of so many companies. The malaise, however, affects public sector organizations too—in education, welfare, and health care, for example.

Our point is that it simply isn't enough to develop a slick organizational mission statement. Rather, the ideal organization will embrace the full implications of authenticity. That is, authenticity in terms of the organization's origins and history, as well as the strongly held individual values that connect to the organization's purpose—both of which we will explore in this chapter.

The fact is that people want to work for an organization that stands for something (something other than shareholder value, that is). Yet authenticity is a complex concept. In recent years much has been written about authenticity as a quality of effective leaders. Indeed, it has become almost an obsession. Some of this literature has come close to arguing that all effective leaders need to do is to "be themselves." However, our work on leadership argues that authenticity is a necessary but insufficient condition for the exercise of leadership.

Similarly, a mission statement cannot alone address authenticity in organizations, as we just pointed out. Such statements became dramatically more popular after the publication of *In Search of Excellence* by Peters and Waterman. High-performance companies, they argued, were typically characterized by a clear idea of what they stood for—they were "hands on, value driven." "Figure out your value system," they wrote. "Decide what your company stands for."[2]

This is not bad advice. The problem comes when the mission statement keeps getting rewritten, as they tend to do. That is when all of an organization's good intentions simply produce cynicism and disbelief, and the mission statement becomes a source of black humor within the company rather than inspiration.

So if a mission statement alone isn't what creates an authentic organization, what does? In this chapter we explore that question and look at the distinct characteristics of authentic organizations and how they can be developed. Our diagnostic toward the chapter's end offers a way to determine how well your organization is already doing on this dimension.

Defining Authenticity

In our research we found three characteristics that seem to consistently differentiate what we regard as authentic organizations: they possess a sense of identity; they obsessively live their values; and their leaders model the company's values.

A Sense of Identity

Roots are important. The *Oxford English Dictionary* defines *authenticity* as "of undisputed origins." Does your organization have identity-defining roots? If so, what are they?

The House of St Barnabas, the London-based nonprofit members-only social club that we introduced in chapter 1, has deeply established roots that give it a unique sense of identity. Begun in 1846 by a wealthy benefactor who effectively gifted his house to a sisterhood of nuns, its mission has always been to support London's homeless. It began this support by keeping poor families together rather than sending them to the workhouse. Over the years, the charity shifted focus and eventually became a hostel for single women. That sense of history supports the club's work today: offering sustained employment for the homeless.

The insurance company New York Life also enjoys a rich sense of history. Founded in 1845, it is one of the largest life insurers in the world. Everything about it—including the building, which occupies a whole block on Madison Avenue and is an official federal and New York City landmark—is solid as a rock. In fact, following the financial crash of 2008, when all was collapsing around it, CEO Ted Mathas announced that New York Life was "built for times like these." The line has stuck because it's true. It stayed safe, it stuck to its principles as a mutual, it didn't make silly bets. New York Life is unusual in that it has the highest possible ratings from all four of the major insurance rating agencies.

When we interviewed Mathas for this book, he acknowledged that mutual status gives his organization an advantage in being able to claim that profit is not the bottom line, and that the company is "here for good." He argues that the same logic applies for public companies—that profit is (or should be) an outcome of the pursuit of other, more meaningful goals: "But many companies in public ownership have lost their way and with it a sense of who they are. New York Life has a 'contrarian' mind-set at the organizational and personal level: a strong sense of . . . who we are and what we should do."

New York Life has recently distilled nine qualities—shared by individual employees and the company as a whole—that it believes ultimately foster New York Life's uniqueness as a workplace. One senior executive described them as "a love poem written after you have been in love." Some extracts:[3]

> Accountability: "You act like an owner of the company—there is no 'they.'"

> Authenticity: "You know who you are and how your actions affect others . . . you question those whose actions appear inconsistent with our values."

Community: "You are loyal to our customers, agents, employees and company . . . you strive to help those in your community."

Conviction: "You never say something you do not mean or do something you fundamentally don't believe in."

Legacy: "You honor and respect the rich history and traditions you have inherited at [the company] . . . you learn and share the traditions, stories and lessons that connect us to our past."

Permanence: "You take positive steps to ensure the permanence and longevity of the company."

But organizations without the longevity of a New York Life or a House of St Barnabas also can be deeply authentic. You don't have to be old to have roots. Apple, whose innovations have transformed telecommunications, mobile computing, music, and entertainment, is one of the darlings of the new digital world. Yet it has a very strong sense of identity indeed, which comes from where it started, who it was up against, and what it was trying to prove. If you ever get the chance to speak to a long-standing Apple executive—and of course despite the youthful image of the company, there are some—he will tell you this story, as he did to one of us. Steve Jobs and Steve Wozniak had just invented the prototype of the Apple Macintosh and they weren't quite sure what to do with it, so they took it to Digital Equipment Company—then the most dominant electronics company in the world. Digital laughed at their silly little invention and told them to hurry back to California. The next day, a delivery arrived at Digital headquarters: a giant wreath with a simple banner that read: "Digital—rest in peace—Apple." The irony of course is that Apple has become one of the world's greatest companies and Digital was swallowed by Compaq. That is the kind of legend that lends an organization a sense of identity.

Some organizations are highly adept at grounding their modernity in tradition, lending them a sense of integrity and authenticity. Sometimes this amalgamation can be physically represented. Consider the following three global training centers. The first is Unilever's Four Acres site situated just outside London. It's an old English country house decorated in Arts and Crafts style with elegant gardens full of traditional English herbaceous borders— it even has a croquet lawn. Its bar has been the focal point of Unilever culture for many years. And yet within this traditional shell, you will find state-of-the-art lecture facilities named after some of Unilever's stunning acquisitions, like Ben and Jerry's, or after some of its powerful global brands, like Dove. The food is healthy and distinctly fusion, expressing perfectly the organization's identity and comfort in a global world. The combination of old and new illustrates Unilever's recognition of its origins as a slightly "clubby" sociable culture and its modern manifestation as a truly global network.

Or visit Credit Suisse's communications center just outside Zurich. You will be greeted upon arrival by a collection of old Swiss farm buildings, in the middle of which stands a high-tech, modern structure. The hospitality is delightfully understated Swiss German. This is, after all, a Swiss bank. The name is not an accident, and yet it is simultaneously an entirely global player. Its Swiss roots, with the emphasis on prudence and good housekeeping, are essential to its value proposition.

Finally, consider Novo Nordisk's new training center at Favrholm. It is built around a two-hundred-year-old Danish farmhouse, and around it and underneath it lie modern facilities designed to stimulate innovation and creativity. The whole building is designed to foster cross-fertilization among the participants, so that R&D, supply chain, sales and marketing, and finance start to see the world through each other's eyes. On one long wall you will find a fascinating pictorial representation of the company's history, demonstrating quite clearly its long-term obsession with improving the lives of diabetics. Even its location is symbolically important: it looks out over an ecologically interesting wetland, beyond which is the factory in Hillerød, which manufactures Novo Nordisk insulin.

All three examples stand in stark contrast to the many faceless training centers that we have visited all over the world. At their worst, too many of those training centers convey nothing of the organizations' history and culture.

Obsessed with Values

Authentic organizations possess a second characteristic feature: they cultivate cultures that are more than a set of words in a value statement and where the brand is more than a slick advertising campaign. Indeed, the brand is, in effect, the external manifestation of the culture.

One way this happens is through corporate purpose. Consider the passion that infuses BMW. The company is stuffed full of very clever German engineers with an obsession for aerodynamics, gearboxes, and engines. Their compulsions are almost tangible. One of the engineers working on the Mini has been known to wake up at four o'clock in the morning to write down an idea that will make the door panels safer. That kind of dedication is shared throughout the company—low-level employees are as knowledgeable about new models as are senior executives. Stop anyone in the corridor at headquarters and ask what BMW is about, and they will speedily answer: "The ultimate driving experience." You immediately sense that this is much more than a slogan to these people. It's an obsession.

Or take an example from an entirely different sector: the natural history unit at the British Broadcasting Corporation. It produces stunning nature programs that are arguably the best of their kind and are broadcast worldwide, such as *The Blue Planet* and *Life on Earth*. Its members are absolutely clear about the unit's purpose and values, so much so that they do not bother to write them down. Indeed, they have little time for the corporate mission statement emanating from the BBC's lofty head offices. They simply want to make the best nature programs in the world. If this means indulging the obsession of a naturalist interested only in the minutiae of moth behavior in the rain forest, then so be it!

Another way in which values are brought alive is through a relentless adherence to standards. As we have already seen at New York Life, standards are everything, for everyone at the company. This is not a company where corners are cut. Things are done the right way and "you act like an owner of the company—there is no 'they.'" So what do you do if you see that standards are not respected? The answer at New York Life, again from its stated nine defining qualities, is clear: "You question those whose actions appear inconsistent with our values." Michael Barry, who has been a field agent for thirty-one years, originally came to the company after abruptly losing his job as a teacher, due to redundancy. "It was a case of last in first out, nothing to do with merit. I decided I never wanted to lose my job like that again . . . That's why I chose New York Life, and I like it more every year. It is a very different company from the top down."

For example, Barry says, the company has deliberately stayed obsessively focused on its core business and turned away from wider financial services when, during a recent era, that was where all the money was. At the time, the agents didn't like it—they felt they were losing money. That is when the CEO at the time, Sy Sternberg, held public forums with the agents, "and no punches were pulled. He told them, 'We are a life insurance company and we are good at it! And we are a mutual, and that's an advantage!'" Barry says that New York Life agents buy into those values wholeheartedly, forming their own study groups, meeting on the weekends. "We are competitors but also friends," he says. Another way that New York Life lives its values is in its commitment to customers. "This is not a place where we wriggle out of claims,"

Barry told us. "One man took out a life policy, went home to write out the check, left it on his desk—and died that night. The policy was unpaid, but we paid the claim."

That same kind of unforgiving focus on standards is also present at Ardbeg, the premium Scotch malt whisky (owned by LVMH), and it's expressed in the way Ardbeg products are developed and brought to market. Lovingly produced by a small staff on the remote island of Islay, the whisky is world renowned for its complex, peaty, yet sweet and smoky flavors. These qualities are no accident. Typically most whiskies are chill-filtered and reduced to a strength of 40 percent alcohol by volume (ABV). Ardbeg Ten Years Old, however, is non-chill-filtered and has a strength of 46 percent ABV, thus retaining maximum flavor while adding increased body and depth. It's no surprise that Ardbeg is a regular whisky industry award winner. And no doubt these achievements result from an unwillingness to compromise on production standards. The obsession with quality has even taken Ardbeg into outer space—to assess the effects of gravity on maturation processes. As Bill Lumsden, director of distilling and whisky creation, explains: "We are always exploring new ways to achieve different taste experiences for our customers. The opportunity to send some Ardbeg spirit and wood into space was truly heaven-sent, and for the first time ever, the effects of micro-gravity on malt whisky maturation is being studied."

Let's look at a last rather different example. Manchester United is not just a soccer team—it's a global business. Its 2014 revenues were forecast as £420-£430 million, which puts it among Europe's biggest sports businesses. But it has a global appeal. The market research firm Kantar recently calculated that Manchester has 659 million adult followers all over the world.[4] It is just about to land the richest sponsorship deal for athletic wear in the history of professional soccer.[5] It is, in short, one of the most successful and valuable franchises in global sport, and its success is based on a rigid adherence to high standards. The team holds itself to obsessively high standards of play, training, and behavior. The whole culture of Manchester United insists on nothing less. Training sessions are focused on intensity, concentration, and speed. The star players—Ronaldo (now of Real Madrid), Beckham (now retired), Scholes—have exemplified these high standards. Nothing sloppy is tolerated.

Finally, the values of a company's culture can emerge through relationships. Consider Heineken, which despite its size (eighty thousand employees) and global scope, retains a distinctive family character. This is no accident. When Freddy Heineken retired from the chairmanship in the mid-1990s, he remarked, "The brewery is like a child to me. Of course, one never really says goodbye to one's child."[6] Another example: when a country manager for Heineken received Freddy Heineken's daughter, Charlene de-Carvalho Heineken, at his business last year, the human connection was immediate. He told us her passion and knowledge of the business was striking, as was her approachability.

At Heineken, the value of family and friends is a strong and recurring feature. Heineken stands for "a long and happy association with good times, good friends and good beer," according to the company literature. At its headquarters, an old Amsterdam house that once served as the Heineken family home, portraits of chairmen past and present decorate the walls. Executives talk of a strong and deep bond with the company—a loyalty and level of participation that means this is more than just a job or a brand.

Heineken's sociable culture fuels a fierce identification with the product and the brand. The friendly atmosphere is everywhere: in the bustling informality of the staff canteen; the regular social events; the family contacts outside work. Of course, the product helps. As one marketer confided to us, "Of course, you realize we don't sell beer—we sell emotional sociability." Friendship at Heineken doesn't just happen; it has its roots in the company's origins, the leadership of its executives, its social routines, its products, and its public relations. When we asked a senior Heineken executive for "success rules" for newly minted company executives, his advice was simple: "Be beery!"

Model Leaders

A final characteristic of authentic organizations is that they have authentic leaders. This may sound like a circular statement of the obvious, and it's true that it can often be difficult to determine which comes first. Let's return to the soccer club example to illustrate this point.

Much of Manchester United's recent success is attributed to the leadership of Sir Alex Ferguson. During his twenty-six years in charge, he became perhaps the most successful coach in all sports. The team won thirteen English League titles and twenty-five other domestic and international trophies. Right from the start, Ferguson saw himself as building a club rather than a particular team. In his words, this involved building from the bottom up. Establishing a strong youth structure was critical for this objective. This meant holding on to a long-term perspective in a notoriously results-driven industry. But Ferguson was prepared to forgo short-term success for long-term achievement. This approach played into something that Ferguson felt fitted the club's early history and culture, which always had been characterized by the development of young players. In the 1950s, that culture was immortalized in the achievements of the legendary "Busby Babes" (as the Manchester United was nicknamed at the time)—a team of outstanding young players, many of whom were tragically killed in what's been called "the Munich air disaster" (a British European Airways crash in February 1958). With his focus on young players, then, Ferguson evoked the past while he worked to build for the future. Not unlike the training centers at Unilever and elsewhere mentioned earlier, Ferguson combined tradition with modernity.

Another example comes from Belmiro de Azevedo, probably Portugal's most famous businessman. We have known Belmiro for many years. He is a formidable personality with a wonderful track record as an entrepreneur, executive, and leader. As we completed this book Belmiro was completing fifty years with Sonae—a highly successful business with interests in retailing, media, information systems, and telecommunications. Belmiro personally embodies many of Sonae's key features: resilient, hardworking, determined, competitive, and focused on performance. We celebrated this winning culture in our earlier book, *The Character of a Corporation*.

Sonae has its origins in wood laminates—a business represented now by Sonae Industria. So where was the commemorative celebration held? In a huge Sonae Industria warehouse especially converted for the occasion. Wooden pallets were the materials for exhibits recording Belmiro's life and achievements. Behind the orchestra on stage, shipping containers were artfully arranged and lit. The several hundred guests included many VIPs—but at Belmiro's table sat only his grandchildren and his wife. The event was a marvelous ritual celebration of authenticity as reflected in exemplary leadership, historic roots, and strong values.

You don't need to be at the top of hierarchies, however, to be a leader who models the kinds of values that underpin authentic organizations. While researching this book, we met a young African American catering manager in a US business school who had been given the daunting task of building a catering outlet, from scratch, that would attract students to work, play, and learn together. She rose to the challenge, and began by focusing her attention on design, colors, space, and furnishings. Then there was the huge challenge of recruiting staff, from chefs to dishwashers, who would live the work-play-and-learn ethos. And she had to design a menu that would connect with the many students concerned with sustainability and health.

It sounds a little schmaltzy, but our observation is that this catering manager wholeheartedly lived all of these values, and lent the outlet a distinctive heart and soul. To visit her space is to witness groups of students discussing politics and philosophy, others hunched over their laptops working on assignments, yet others playing board games, and some just laughing with each other. She radiates energy through work, through fun and through constant dialogues with staff and customers. With her unique ability as leader to model the values she hopes to instill, she has succeeded in creating an authentic space in which staff as well as students and faculty do indeed work, play, and learn together.

In a very different place—China—a businesswoman named Dong Mingzhu has transformed Gree (a manufacturer of air-conditioning units) from a sleepy domestic brand into a world leader with sales exceeding $10 billion. The company continues to grow rapidly, with manufacturing facilities developed in Brazil, Pakistan, and Vietnam. The youngest of seven children born into a humble working family, Dong worked her way through the Gree hierarchy from junior sales agent to chief executive. Her success has not been without sacrifice. With a legendary commitment to her work, Dong hasn't taken a holiday in twenty years. Even when her husband died some years back, she left her three-year-old son with his grandmother in Nanjing to continue dedicating herself to building Gree. Visits back to her son came only when business brought her to the city. The story goes that later, when the twelve-year-old son visited her, she refused to give him a lift back to the airport and forbade anyone else to do so. He took the bus. She also refused her brother a discount when he wanted preferential terms to run a Gree dealership. They didn't speak for many years.

Are we saying that an organization with authenticity must also have an austere leader? Not necessarily. But sometimes, and especially in a culture such as China's, a leader who sets an extremely strict personal example wins huge respect from employees. As one of her forty thousand employees—a devoted sales manager—put it: "She's been through everything herself. We never dare to say that something is impossible in front of her. We must all have her will to succeed." Yet Dong's reputation is not all about toughness. Her care for her employees is reflected in the fact that, for example, women receive twice the normal levels of Chinese maternity leave. Dong is, in effect, an exemplar of what we called "tough empathy" in our book *Why Should Anyone Be Led by You?*: a hard-edged kind of caring that is reciprocated and mirrored by her own employees.[7]

All the examples we have cited so far are unambiguously positive in their outcomes for employees and customers. But inevitably there are risks. Leaders who authentically demonstrate the values of an organization will not always produce businesses that are universally admired—even if they are economically successful. What's more, if values are tied excessively to one powerful individual, the organization may be very difficult to change without replacing that person.

Consider Michael O'Leary, the tough, no-nonsense boss of Ryanair, the no-frills budget airline that has become one of Europe's largest. Ryanair's success is based on a simple proposition that its prices will be the lowest. But historically there were hefty add-on charges should you decide to select an allocated seat, fail to arrive with a printed boarding pass, or any number of other "offenses." And you did not expect a free drink or snack on board—everything had an extra charge. Though the company remains successful, the ruthless application of add-ons resulted in a distinctly mixed reputation with customers, whose resentments became a source of black humor. Yet O'Leary remained unrepentant, renowned for publicly belittling his customers for their unrealistic expectations of a pared-back budget service. Cheap is what they bought—cheap is (authentically) what they got.

The culture of the airline comes absolutely from the pugnacious character of its chief executive. It has worked up until now. But things can change, and the ability of competitors to compare on price and yet deliver higher levels of service has forced Ryanair to explicitly attempt a makeover toward a more customer-friendly experience. Whether Ryanair can achieve this with O'Leary as chief executive is an interesting question. How far can he change without himself appearing to lose his authenticity? The early signs are fairly positive—both shareholders and customers are happier.

But as we have argued elsewhere, authenticity isn't about being the same all the time. Heineken is a case in point. Earlier we talked about the company's highly sociable culture, which its leader, Freddy Heineken, had really understood. A few years later, a tough Dutchman, Karel Vursteen, was brought in as the company's CEO. At his previous position at Philips North America, he had developed a reputation as a highly successful turnaround executive. His view when he arrived at Heineken was that it had become a little complacent and sleepy and needed to wake up to the changing dynamics of the global beer market. So he modeled a kind of tough distance—constantly talking about the strength of the competition, of giants like Anheuser-Busch who could disrupt the cozy world of Heineken. The message got through. Heineken reaffirmed its position as a globally competitive beer producer, and Vursteen could allow his deep love of beer and sociability to appear again. He was a regular visitor to the delightful bar at the Heineken head office where executives met at the end of the day to bounce ideas off each other.

What Organizations Can Do

We've now looked at some of the characteristics of organizations that put authenticity at their core. The diagnostic in the sidebar, "Does Your Organization Stand for Authenticity?," offers a quick check on whether you work for an authentic company.

In response to the diagnostic questions, participants from both high- and low-discretion jobs show the same pattern. They tend

Diagnostic: Does Your Organization Stand for Authenticity?

1 = Strongly Disagree   2 = Disagree   3 = Neither Agree Nor Disagree
4 = Agree   5 = Strongly Agree

_____ I know what we stand for.

_____ I value what we stand for.

_____ I want to exceed my current duties.

_____ Profit is not our overriding goal.

_____ I am accomplishing something worthwhile.

_____ I like to tell people where I work.

Consider any statement to which you assign a 1 or 2 as worth your sustained attention. An overall score below 18 suggests that this area of your organizational life requires improvement. Ask yourself how long you will give the organization to make genuine progress.

to score a little better on the first and last items, but they are least convinced that "profit is not our overriding goal."

Although each of the diagnostic statements implies an important organizational and leadership imperative, let's be clear: in the domain of authenticity, there are no quick fixes. We cannot supply you with a list of the five things that you must do to ensure that your organization is authentic. We should stress that building an authentic organization requires patience and resilience—indeed, a certain kind of single-mindedness. In fact, one caveat we'd like to offer is that small start-up businesses may have a better chance at authenticity than large bureaucratic organizations. And even small or start-up companies must be cautious as they enter the travails of high-growth business (such as cash flow problems) that they are not forced to renege on their values.

One general observation of the positive examples cited in this chapter is that these organizations are suspicious of the fads and fashions that sweep organizational life. They are often characterized by a kind of contrarian mind-set. They are very clear about what they do well and are unlikely to be convinced by passing trends that are insufficiently thought through. This does not mean they might not recognize the need for change or are unable to manage change.

So, despite our hesitation in offering "to-dos" when it comes to authenticity, we have found three tasks for companies that seem to follow from the examples of the authentic organizations we observed: be vigilant, acknowledge legacy, and think about the connections between the personal and the organizational.

Be Vigilant

Authentic organizations seem to keep checking their values and the manner in which they are applied. (This corresponds to "Profit is not our overriding goal" and "I am accomplishing something worthwhile" in the diagnostic.) When we worked with Johnson & Johnson, for example, we witnessed firsthand a consultant being publicly reprimanded for acting in a manner deemed inconsistent with the J&J credo that encapsulates their values. We were taken aback, but soon came to realize that this is a company that really does take its values seriously. We came to appreciate the huge significance of the Credo workshops, which are designed to allow employees to regularly discuss, critique, and apply company values. J&J can be regarded as exemplary in the consistency between preaching and practice, but it is never satisfied that things are perfect. The time, expense, and effort of regular Credo workshops continue to be regarded as a useful investment. Remember, too, the organizational audit processes at Novo Nordisk, where seasoned executives regularly visit affiliate organizations to ensure that they are fully following the Novo Nordisk Way. This system has now become so embedded in the culture that it is regarded as a positive source of feedback rather than intrusive control from the center.

Acknowledge Legacy

This imperative links to "I know what we stand for" and "I value what we stand for" in the diagnostic. But understanding your origins doesn't just happen. What we discovered from our research is that authentic organizations work hard at their own history— whether long or short. This may be physically symbolized, such as in the training centers of Novo Nordisk, Credit Suisse, and Unilever. Or it can be verbally expressed and seen as an explicit requirement for employees. Recall that New York Life expects its people to "respect the rich history and traditions you have inherited at [the company] . . . you learn and share the traditions, stories, and lessons that connect us to our past." One of the most exciting and innovative pharma companies of recent times is Genentech, which has developed life-changing drugs like Avastin and Herceptin. It's a young company but its legacy is already strong. When you encounter former Genentech employees elsewhere in the industry, they always speak highly of their time working with the company.

Think Hard about the Connections between the Personal and the Organizational

This corresponds to the statements in the diagnostic, "I like to tell people where I work" and "I want to exceed my current duties" (i.e., when you invest your authentic self in your work, you become more than your job description). Just as C. Wright Mills in his classic book *The Sociological Imagination* reminded us, human beings are empowered by seeing the connection between biography and history, between ill-defined private troubles and public issues.[8] These are juxtapositions that enable us all to become full citizens—knowledgeable and intentional in our public lives. This brings to mind an interesting question we had recently from a global HR task force at Samsung, set up to investigate the "nature of virtue." Why, the task force was asking, do we teach children at school to be virtuous, then forget about it entirely when they grow up and begin work? Our view is that as we seek to build authentic organizations, more and more companies must engage with these difficult questions.

In the next chapter, we discuss the issue of meaning at work. Our contention is that in the organization of your dreams, work is meaningful in an organization that itself has meaning.

Action Points for Leaders

✔ **Demonstrate your own authenticity.** You can hardly expect this in others if you don't demonstrate it yourself. As we have urged repeatedly in our earlier research: be yourself—more—with skill. This means understanding what you have in terms of the distinctive personal differences that can work positively for you, as well as the weaknesses that may effectively humanize you. With this self-insight it is then possible to explore what works in particular contexts and particular relationships. Remember, the skillful communication of authenticity rests upon an expert read of your situation.

✔ **Understand your personal authentic roots.** Organizations have roots and so do you. It is inauthentic to attempt to write these off, but in a mobile world some people try. Search for a balance between where you started and where you are now. Clearly you need to adapt to where you work in order to make connections. But too much conformity and you will lose your individuality and leadership ability; not enough and you will never produce sustainable change.

✔ **Communicate what you stand for and what you take pride in—clearly and simply.** Use opportunities to connect this communication to organizational purpose and values. Tell personal stories—they can be very effective. The most powerful value systems can be deduced from real behavior—they don't have to be written down.

✔ **Get authenticity feedback from others.** Colleagues can be really good at spotting the drift into inauthenticity. But if you're near the top of your organization, remember that much of the feedback you receive has already been carefully filtered. Be prepared to find out what's really going on.

Chapter 5

Make It Meaningful

Ensuring the Daily Work Is Intrinsically Satisfying

Certainly, employees need a sense of shared meaning and understanding about the mission and purpose of the company's work. That is what workplaces that embody authenticity are all about, as we saw in the last chapter. But the people we have spoken with also long for work that is intrinsically satisfying, meaningful in itself. After all, if as adults we spend most of our waking life at work, it had better be a place that provides meaningful activity. This has led us to a rather different take on the conventional question about work–life balance. Work is a defining human characteristic, and without it, life itself loses some of its meaning. The typical "balanced life" solution—to spend more time at home and fewer hours in the office—doesn't begin to address the need for meaning. As founder Ove Arup stated it in his "Key Speech" to executives back in 1970:

There are two ways of looking at the work you do to earn a living. One is the way propounded by the late Henry Ford: work is a necessary evil, but modern technology will reduce it to a minimum. Your life is your leisure lived in your "free" time. The other is: to make your work interesting and rewarding. You enjoy both your work and your leisure. We opt uncompromisingly for the second way.[1]

Or, as legendary author and radio journalist Studs Terkel put it:

Work is about daily meaning as well as daily bread; for recognition as well as cash, in short, for a sort of life rather than a Monday-through-Friday sort of dying . . . We have a right to ask of work that it include meaning, recognition, astonishment and life![2]

The ideal organization provides intrinsically meaningful work, the likes of which go far beyond simple job enrichment add-ons. It is work that connects one person's job to others, and it resists workplace cultures that overcontrol and alienate. This requires nothing less than a deliberate reconsideration of the tasks each person is performing. Do those duties make sense? Why are they what they are? Are they as engaging as they could be?

This is a huge, complex undertaking. In fact, there are libraries full of research on where and how humans find meaning in work.[3] Alain de Botton, the social philosopher, summarizes it simply like this: meaning comes from either increasing pleasure or reducing pain. Serve great food or sell a wonderful car, and you increase customer pleasure. Provide groundbreaking medical services and you reduce pain. De Botton has actually asked people what their ideal job would be. The most common answer? Running a small guest house or a local shop of some kind. What these two places share is a clear connection between job and outcome—you can see immediately and clearly the benefit and pleasure that others gain from your efforts (and by extension, as research shows, the pleasure you gain from providing pleasure to others).[4]

Case in point: While we were doing the fieldwork for this book we spent many tiring days interviewing employees in London—often long, arduous days! They were made more bearable by discovering a little bar run by two Irishmen from County Cork. The bar would be full and sweat would be dripping from the Irishmen's chins as they served pint after pint of Guinness to quench the thirst of beleaguered city workers. During a rare, slightly quieter moment at the bar, we asked them what it was like working in this very busy establishment. In a delightful Irish brogue one replied, insightfully, "It's grand—there's nothing like pouring a perfect pint of Guinness for customers who really look like they need it. At the end of a full-on couple of hours, I feel tired but strangely happy." Perhaps not surprisingly, it's also a very profitable business.

Returning to De Botton's work, we see that his concern with the pursuit of pleasure and the avoidance of pain taps into a major theme of Western philosophy. It connects hard-hitting utilitarianism—with its insistence that the rightness of an action be judged by how much it increases human happiness or decreases misery—with more modern existential notions, which insist on individual responsibility for happiness. As Albert Camus succinctly put it, "Life is the sum of your choices."

That quote seems particularly fitting in a book that attempts to answer, Why should anyone work here? If it's true that today's organizations must work harder to get the best people to *choose them* (rather than the other way around), then providing jobs that are meaningful in themselves is essential to attracting employees and inspiring them to do their best work.

In this chapter, we will discuss why for some people work can feel devoid of meaning, and sometimes mind-numbing. We will examine sources of meaning that people find in their jobs—specifically the way their jobs connect them to others, their work's location within a wider community, and how their job relates to an overall organizational cause. Finally, our diagnostic will help you determine the level of meaning your organization offers its people, followed by specific suggestions for how to improve.

What Makes Work Meaningless?

As de Botton shows, three causal factors help answer this question. The first of these is *scale*. Large corporations can be so massive that connecting individual work to outcomes becomes difficult. If we examine the history of work since the industrial revolution, we see that over time, capitalism tends to result in an ever-increasing concentration of wealth and resources. Thus, we witnessed the rise of giant corporations. This process was spectacularly swift in the United States because rates of capital accumulation were much faster than in other parts of the world, leading enlightened capitalists like Frank A. Seiberling and Paul W. Litchfield of Goodyear Tire and Rubber Co. to warn in the 1920s that the modern corporation was in danger of running out of control and becoming responsible only to itself. In the light of recent scandals, that observation seems remarkably prescient. Karl Marx put it rather more brutally: "One capitalist kills many." Of course, one of the reasons for capitalism's continuing relative health is that, while it is concentrated at the top, it is also sucking in new competition at the bottom. That's why capitalism remains the most successful social and economic system the world has ever seen. It's interesting to observe that today, at the moment of its deepest crisis since 1929, capitalism has no significant rivals.

And yet the massive structures and wealth that capitalism produces don't always result in a rich day-to-day work experience. Even in Silicon Valley, which cultivated a series of start-ups and job growth a few decades ago (think Apple, Google, and Oracle), capitalism's modern ecology is simply not the same today. There are still many start-ups, of course, but they are often clients of the giants like Google and Apple, which increasingly dominate their sectors. We may conclude that despite the cyclical nature of economic growth, scale continues to be a feature of the modern organization—with enormous consequences for work itself. Scale is not just a characteristic of manufacturing—though of course we saw it in the rise of Bethlehem Steel, DuPont, Tata, Sony, and Ford. It is also a feature of white-collar work. Remember Charlie Chaplin's wonderful silent film *Modern Times*, with its serried ranks of clerks? More recently the alienation of white-collar workers was comically captured in the TV sitcom *The Office*. Scale has increasingly become a feature of service operations, too. Any visit to a call center provides ample testimony to this.

The major problem with scale, of course, is that it breeds elaborate hierarchies and increasingly pervasive bureaucratic control systems. On the one hand, this inhibits the expression of individual differences (discussed in chapter 1) and on the other, it creates a miasma of rules that curtail innovation and creativity (a theme we will develop in chapter 6).

Linked with scale is a second reason work often feels meaningless: the emergence of an extensive *division of labor* as tasks become broken down into more easily measured and controllable elements. Connecting these individual parts to a definable product or service becomes more challenging. There have been many attempts in modern corporations to counter these forces for job fragmentation through a variety of job rotation, job enrichment, and employee engagement strategies. But they have met with mixed success. To quote the factory worker in a classic piece of British industrial sociology: "You move from one boring monotonous job to another boring, dirty, monotonous job and somehow you're supposed to come out of it all 'enriched.' But I never feel 'enriched'—I just feel knackered."[5]

A third reason for the sense of disconnection that often prevails in the workplace relates to the difficulties created by *time lags*. In the small guest house or corner store, the customer impact of your efforts is directly and quickly experienced. But in a large global pharmaceutical company, for example, connecting an individual job to a customer experience becomes a major challenge when an individual's work on a complex chemical compound only translates into a usable product some seven years later. The syndrome is reflected in the abstract—sometimes bizarre—nature of modern occupational titles. Ask a new acquaintance what she does and you open a minefield. What exactly is a "leadership and learning strategy engagement adviser" or a "matrix strategy systems integrator"? Such titles leave us shaking our heads, wondering what the person actually produces or does, and how the job relates to a consumer or customer.

Organizations' attempts to address this pathology of disconnect (bred by time lags) include "meet the customer campaigns" or chief executives who vow to spend one day per week on the shop floor. In the main these attempts fail—they are abandoned because people are too busy. Think about it—how many people in your organization ever consistently meet customers?

What Makes Work Meaningful?

But perhaps we are being too gloomy. Sure, there are powerful forces that produce alienation, but we remain committed to the view that work is central to a satisfying human existence. We also know that human beings are remarkably creative at snatching meaning and pleasure from some pretty unpromising circumstances. The US industrial anthropologist Donald Roy, writing in the late 1940s, studied machine shop operatives in Chicago.[6] He was among the first to adopt a participant-observation approach to shop floor workers. These workers were subject to the worst excesses of Taylorism and payment-by-piece rates—unpromising territory indeed for creativity and meaning. Yet Roy shows that the workers used enormous ingenuity to short-circuit the piece-rate system and to find novel ways of making things while ignoring the carefully crafted Taylorist blueprints. They even found a way to control time! One of Roy's most entertaining and insightful articles is called "Banana Time."[7] It chronicles the ways in which the workers used the ritual consumption of fruit to break up the day and give it meaning. Interestingly, this research found an almost direct analogue in the work of Hungarian sociologist Miklos Haraszti, who in his book *Worker in a Worker's State* describes similar processes under conditions of state socialism (it's worth remembering that Lenin was a great admirer of Frederick Winslow Taylor!).[8]

There is now widespread evidence that employees, even in low-discretion jobs, can be very creative. In any event, you will be surprised what people find meaningful. Fish gutting is regularly ranked at the top of the list of most unpopular jobs. Yet in his book *Working*, Studs Terkel reveals how one worker makes the fabulous observation that the guts "feel like velvet." It is dangerous to impose on others your own assumptions about what is meaningful. There are barmen who clearly take pride in pouring the perfect pint; baristas who are meticulous about the production of their cappuccino; even airline check-in staff who refuse to treat you as a number. All these individuals are resolutely refusing to be restricted by the limits of their role. Clever organizations have recognized this potential in their employees and designed jobs that allow individuals greater scope for self-expression. As Dov Seidman has recently observed in his discussion of the relative weight of rules and values and the possibilities of self-governance, to inspire your employees, you may need to set them free.[9]

Consider Barclaycard, the payments arm of the Barclays group, which runs many large call centers. To help employees deliver great service by better responding to customers' individual situations, while empowering them to create an emotional connection with customers, "magic moments" were introduced. Magic moments allow employees the discretion to make a customer's day through small acts of kindness. For example, if a customer calls to explain a late payment because his partner has just given birth after a long and arduous labor, the employee could give them a grace period to make their payment—and send a bouquet of flowers or other small gift to the new mother. It's a lovely idea—with a relatively small budget set aside to fund it. Initially, employees were reluctant to use the "moments," fearing sanction from above or that they would bust the budget. It took skilled leadership to create a culture where call-center employees felt able and willing to use discretion.

More to the point, finding meaning in one's work also emerges from what we have called the three Cs—connection, community, and cause. Employees need to know how their work connects to others' work (especially when silos get in the way). They need a workplace that promotes a sense of belonging (increasingly difficult in a mobile world). And they need to know how their work contributes to a longer-term goal (problematic, when shareholders demand quarterly reporting). If these issues are not addressed, any efforts to "engage" employees will produce temporary improvement at best.

One workplace we know of that exemplifies all three Cs is London's House of St Barnabas (HoSB), mentioned in previous chapters. At HoSB, meaningful work is practically built into the DNA of the nonprofit members-only social club that supports London's homeless by providing jobs. Says CEO Sandra Schembri about her own search for meaningful work: "I was looking for more than just, 'Can I do the job?' I was looking for a place with potential to make a difference. HoSB provides that . . . [the work] is absolutely captivating."

Let's look now at connection, community, and cause and how each functions to infuse people's jobs with meaning.

Meaning from Connection

Meaning derives not just from the job we're doing. Connections matter. The use of the word *connect* here is significant; it implies relationships. Yet much of the classic research of meaning at work is profoundly individualistic. It arrives at a satisfaction score in terms of a calculus between individuals and their work. Connection forces us to look at the nexus of social relationships in which most work is located.

Even where connections can be made and individuals derive meaning from relationships, that does not necessarily lead to a constructive contribution to the organization's purpose. A silo mentality is only too familiar in many organizations where the solidarity of the sales team is at least partially generated by their collective distrust of the manufacturing function—and their mutual disrespect of headquarters.

Silos are an old problem. We were shocked to find, in fact, just how much the problems created by deeply ingrained silo mentalities persist among some organizations that we studied for this book. Too often, the connections between research and development, between compliance and sales, between sales and marketing remain characterized by mistrust, negative politics, and of course suboptimal organizational outcomes. We see this at work in pharmaceutical companies and in the continuing tensions between front and back office in our major financial institutions. As we write this book, the future of Time Warner once more seems uncertain. Its central issue for the recent past has been an inability to fully exploit synergies among its various businesses. It's remarkable how intractable some of these issues can be. At the heart of the problem is the paradox of team building—when you build strong teams you may exclude others. Thus it becomes a leadership imperative, as you build a strong team, to also build the connection to adjacent functions and the wider organization.

We encountered one example of this when we were working with a high-potential sales manager in a fast-moving consumer goods company in Malaysia. She exemplified the kind of driven young executive characteristically found in emerging markets. She quickly captured the techniques of team building, devoted time to it, and before long, she had captured the hearts and minds of her team. Only several years later did she start to realize that the team ethos she had created was impeding proper relationships with both marketing and supply-chain management. At an organizational level, these problems manifested themselves in a blame culture, where problems were always the fault of someone else. She told us: "I realized that much of the effort I had put into team building—which I really enjoyed—hadn't been directed at what the real organizational issues were. I needed to think more about how you stitch the whole thing together."

One way to address silo issues has been the rise of complex matrix structures. As we discussed in chapter 2, matrices typically emerge in knowledge-intensive, complex businesses with increasing numbers of highly qualified, specialized employees. Those workers' major focus is their narrow field of expertise and they are often, potentially, a source of significant added value. In another book, we called these people "clevers." They are smart, talented, and highly motivated. But they are also difficult—they can be self-obsessed, resistant to (negative) feedback, and highly individualistic. Their self-identity comes primarily from their occupation rather than their organization, and they are therefore well networked externally and potentially highly mobile. Their increasing numbers in modern corporations are another reason why it can be difficult to create and sustain meaningful long-term organizational relationships.

Different kinds of connections can be made with, for example, suppliers or customers. At the British food retailer Waitrose, buyers derive meaning by building long-term connections with their suppliers. One senior food buyer put it like this: "We have relationships of respect with our suppliers; we demand high standards of them and they of us. But over time I found that I treat them like members of a sort of extended family. I would certainly go out of my way to help them, and I'd like to think they'd do the same for me."

Meaning from Community

Meaning also comes from building a sense of community and belonging in organizations—and gaining a sense of meaning in work itself. But this has not been helped by the changing shape of work life. Specifically, conventional career spans have become shorter over time and more mobile. Some years back, Charles Handy encapsulated these changes in an intriguing arithmetic.[10] He described the typical corporate career from the 1950s onward as comprising "three 47s": 47 hours a week, 47 weeks a year, and 47 years. This calculated out to a 100,000-hour lifetime of employment. Moreover, these hours often took place within the confines of a single organization. Organizations such as Exxon, IBM, Unilever, and Sony were full of lifetime "corporate men" (women at the time were rarely able to sustain the continuity required by these careers).

Handy's claim was that employment careers were, in the last decades of the twentieth century, becoming shorter—nearer 50,000 hours—and more mobile. This change came as a result of various socioeconomic shifts, including employer needs for flexibility, lengthening periods in education, and employee expectations of work–life balance. Simple arithmetic shows that 50,000 hours could be achieved through three 37s ($37 \times 37 \times 37$). For hardpressed executives and professionals, typically the 50,000 hours are achieved by working 60 hours a week, 50 weeks a year, over a 17-year period. These 17 years increasingly occur, with a more well-educated work force, from the age of around twenty-eight through to the midforties—by which time individuals have either made it or they haven't.

Further, it is not unusual for individuals to move among several organizations during this 17-year period. In effect, career patterns have moved from a steady 47-year jog through one corporate hierarchy to an intensive sprint across several. Arguably, these patterns have intensified since Handy offered his predictions. It is not unusual for companies to compete for highly talented MBA students who have completed three years with McKinsey, knowing that once they have them, they will be lucky to hang onto them for three years. But in those three years the companies will likely benefit from very high levels of performance; these individuals can make a difference.

While these contrasting employment patterns each have their pros and cons, clearly today's shorter and more mobile patterns present challenges in terms of creating long-term organizational attachments. The old career provided a continuity of experience, where slow movement up an elaborate hierarchy generated meaning for individuals. The three 47s were a significant source of cohesion and loyalty. They were the base upon which the "organization man" was crafted. Social critics like Richard Sennett, in his book *The Corrosion of Character*, argue that this new form of "flexible" capitalism has profound negative consequences for workers and for society. His book ends with this rather eloquent and disturbing observation: "[A] regime which provides human beings no deep reasons to care about one another cannot long preserve its legitimacy."[11] So the new challenge becomes *how to create strong identification within short bursts of employment.* The reality in many organizations, of course, is that new patterns mix with old legacies. It is not unusual, therefore, to see older employees who still approximate the three 47s pattern working alongside younger, more mobile colleagues.

Between the older corporate loyalists and the younger mobile "talent" sit a burgeoning group of part-time employees. Originally, Handy alluded to these predominantly (at the time) female workers through another distinctive arithmetic: 25 hours a week by 25 weeks a year over 50 years. The problem, of course, is that such part-time, poorly paid, and typically female employees are never wealthy enough to retire! In the contemporary labor market, it is possible to see these patterns in even more extreme forms— witness the dramatic growth of zero-hour contracts. These have become popular in certain sectors of the UK economy over recent years—in retailing, hotels, and catering, for example—and effectively put employees "on call" for work but allow employers the option of offering nothing. Building a cohesive, meaningful team—let alone corporate community—when it is characterized by a fragmented arithmetic is a demanding task.

It is worth saying that even people working the $60 \times 50 \times 17$ pattern might never actually stop working in their lifetimes. Advances in the pharmaceutical industry mean that we will likely be living longer. Pension schemes face serious difficulties, so we will all probably be working more years than we'd thought. The problem, of course, is that our careers will be "over" for longer too—we will have more working years left after having reached the pinnacles of our careers. HR professionals have been arguing for some time that careers peak earlier. Well, if they do, something follows as a mathematical necessity. You will be plateaued for longer—if you stay. The potential lack of novelty and motivation implied by that fact is hard to fathom. At the very least it removes a major source of meaning.

All of these shifts in employment patterns combine to make a feeling of community at work harder to achieve. But there is also a wider argument that in the Western world, there is a more widespread affiliation gap as the things we used to identify with—religion, class, and political party—all become weaker. A rather gloomy conclusion may be that we are increasingly isolated in the pressure cooker of our nuclear families. Hardly a recipe for sustained mental health.

But what kind of community do we want? Here comes a really difficult intellectual challenge. The concept of community is one of the most elusive in modern social science, despite its centrality to much of what we might think about work and society. Part of the problem lies in its ubiquity—listen to the language of modern politics—community schools, community hospitals, community sports clubs. When a term is used so loosely it becomes increasingly difficult to know what it really means. We have previously argued that community is made up of two types of relationship.[12] The first is *sociability*—noninstrumental relationships with an affective component. You might more colloquially call this friendship, but of course, friendship is the most commonly occurring human relationship, as well as being the one we understand the least.

Just for a moment, think about your own friendship network—old friends, new friends, male friends, female friends, sports friends, work friends, church friends, political friends, bar friends. You see, friendship is complicated, but is an essential ingredient of community. Indeed, we would make the prediction that sociability will make a comeback at work. Organizations whose modus operandi has devolved largely into remote, mobile working relationships will be reinstating shared coffee areas and eating places, which once facilitated sociable relations at work.[13] High levels of sociability at work fuel higher levels of creativity as we bounce ideas off each other, higher levels of enjoyment since we like working with our friends, and higher levels of effort as we seek to support those we like.

We have termed the second social relationship found in communities *solidarity*—instrumental relationships based on a strong sense of shared interests. You don't have to like certain colleagues to realize that they are very good at their job and vital to your collective success. Yet solidarity—unlike sociability, which exists over time—is contingent and intermittent. That is to say, it is produced at moments when we perceive our shared interests. At work, high levels of solidarity gives us focus, the ability to move quickly, and a well-developed sense of the equality of suffering. That is to say, if we lose, we all lose.

Where levels of both sociability and solidarity are high we can describe the organizational culture as communal—think Apple, Google, Virgin, Island Records, and many small family businesses. These cultures are characterized by employees' passion for what they do, high levels of loyalty, and a tendency to obsession. Work is life and life is work. Cultures are significant suppliers of meaning. In contrast, think of organizations that are both low on sociability and solidarity. Some of these are elite academic institutions like the top business schools; indeed, when we interviewed professors at a top US B-school they said, essentially, "I go to work to be alone." And yet Stanford and Harvard are not entirely devoid of a sense of community. They provide meaning through endowing elite status and reputation on their members.

Of course, one of the huge issues that we collectively face is how to make sense of the exponential growth of the internet and its capacity to connect people digitally. Many have argued that the growth of online communities more than compensates for the decline in traditional communities. We are stubbornly agnostic on this point, but would raise the following slightly skeptical notes on the efficacy of online communities. If you ask a group of people whether they have tried internet dating, you will get the following response. The men, in the main, tightly fold their arms to indicate that of course they have no such need, while a few brave women will put up their hands. We then begin to explore some of the problems and issues with internet dating. They are, in a nutshell, that prospective partners usually have to meet—they have to "eyeball" each other, smile or grimace.

Our simple point is this—that we are hard wired for face-to-face communication. It is ironic that in a television documentary about Facebook, even Mark Zuckerberg's day-to-day managerial style at corporate HQ relies on face-to-face contact—what used to be called "management by wandering around."[14] It is equally true that the digital world is brilliant at connecting what you might call "communities of interest"—the seed swappers of Cincinnati, the stamp collectors of Seattle. This explains why our security services track internet traffic so carefully—for it is not just stamp collectors who connect this way, but also terrorist organizations.

Meaning from Working for a Cause

We've explored how work is more meaningful when it gives us a sense of connection to others as well as to the community at large. But meaning also comes from identification with a cause. Without a strong overarching goal to work for, people may defect. When work becomes a cause, it is likely to be more meaningful, as it is for the engineers at BMW and the agents at New York Life.

But we also acknowledge an element of risk when it comes to such "causes." When we interviewed legendary games designer Will Wright, he told us that his primary affiliation was not with his company, Electronic Arts (EA), but with the project or cause associated with it. For him, originally that was the record-breaking Sims game franchise and subsequently the groundbreaking development of Spore. "You say Electronic Arts, but to me that doesn't have much meaning," he said when we interviewed him. Will Wright subsequently left EA to restart afresh independently. So keeping the cause in-house can be a challenge, similar to that of fostering personal growth. If you don't do it, the best people may leave or never consider you at all. Or your competitors may develop the potential in people you've overlooked. When you do make the investment, your staff members become more valuable to you.

The leaders' role, then, is to identify the source of the cause *within the organization*. Ted Mathas, chairman and CEO at New York Life, recently led a brand-positioning exercise that revealed how strongly employees identified "in their bones" the company as a "force for good" in protecting its clients. In their terms, "profit is not our bottom line"—the cause is to keep families together and "to keep widows on their porches" rather than losing their homes after the death of a spouse.

As we argued in the last chapter, *the* most significant source of meaning for talented people comes from a shared cause or sense of purpose. Steve Varley is chairman of EY in the UK. After reporting record profits and partners earnings during his first year in the role, Steve put a question to his senior partners at his inaugural conference: "Is that all there is?" He used this question and the occasion to launch an initiative aimed at achieving growth and social change, called "Growing Successfully, Making the Difference." In his eyes, these socially oriented but business-connected activities were an important way to differentiate his firm and to better position it to attract and retain talent. It is interesting to see that EY's recently adopted global mission, "building a better working world," plays to exactly the same theme and has been launched by all countries in which EY operates, including the UK and Ireland.

What is clear from those examples is that attempting to understand the meaningful purpose of business enterprise purely through narrow financial or economic criteria misses the point. For example, telephone conversations we've overheard at companies over the past thirty-odd years include the following:

> "I'll be home late, darling—we are working on a cure for migraine."

> "Still at work—the new U2 album comes out tomorrow."

> "Sorry, a colleague has a presentation to the CEO—I'm helping him run the numbers."

> "Very busy on the plan to take insulin into East Africa."

And yet, we've never heard this:

> "I'll be home late—I'm increasing shareholder value."

Perhaps it's worth restating the simple point that the most profitable enterprises are *not* the most profit oriented. Read Jack Welch, James Collins, Jerry Porras, or John Kay and you will find that consistently high-performing organizations are driven by obsessions relating to, for example, product, service, quality, innovation, and, yes, fun—and it is these that in turn seem to drive successful financial performance. Kay, for example, points to the success of ICI when its purpose was chemical science; Boeing when it was driven by making great planes; and Merck when its focus was medicine for the people. Subsequent changes in ownership and leadership led all three to take profit, shareholder value, and growth as priorities—with negative consequences in each case.[15]

What Organizations Can Do

In the sidebar, "How Meaningful Is Your Work?," you'll find the diagnostic we use to assess just how meaningful people find their jobs.

Overall, executives' responses to the questions on meaning are the most positive compared with the other diagnostic sections. This is true for both high- and low-discretion jobs. Perhaps this is the case for two reasons. First, organizations have made big efforts in this area. Second, it is testament to the human capacity to eke out meaning from the most unpromising circumstances.[16] However, there is more to be done. The diagnostic questions imply some possible initiatives for leaders and organizations alike for instilling a sense of meaning into people's jobs. Here are some suggestions.

Organize around Enthusiasms

This imperative connects to our diagnostic statement "My work gives me energy and pleasure." Yet organizing around people's enthusiasms is a deceptively simple idea; it is hard to put into operation. Its origins are in anarchist theories of work that portray hierarchies, systems, and procedures as obstacles to individuals'

Diagnostic: How Meaningful Is Your Work?

1 = Strongly Disagree   2 = Disagree   3 = Neither Agree Nor Disagree
4 = Agree   5 = Strongly Agree

_____ My job is meaningful to me.

_____ My duties make sense to me.

_____ My work gives me energy and pleasure.

_____ I understand how my job fits with everyone else's.

_____ Everyone's job is necessary.

_____ At work we share a common cause.

Consider any statement to which you assign a 1 or 2 as worth your sustained attention. An overall score below 18 suggests that this area of your organizational life requires improvement. Ask yourself how long you will give the organization to make genuine progress.

full expressions of themselves at work. You do not have to embrace all of this to accept the idea that around their enthusiasms people connect with emotions, and emotions are major sources of energy at work.

This is as true for science-based companies like GlaxoSmith-Kline and sophisticated engineering firms like BMW as it is for more obvious examples like Louis Vuitton. But when we work with executives, they sometimes say, "It's all very well for you two—you work with creative businesses like pharmaceutical companies and media companies. I'm in insurance—my business is boring." Our riposte? "What's insurance really about? It's about having your roof repaired in time for Christmas, making good on flood damage, getting a courtesy car after a road accident— insurance is really exciting!"

Consider the following examples:

- One of the authors of this book has patronized the same bank since our student days (and believe us, that's a long time). Like many customers, he's long been dissatisfied with the bank's performance, so much so that his partner, fed up from hearing complaints, presented him with the forms to close his account. The author's passionate protest? "I can't move now—I couldn't let Mrs. G down." Despite the bank's poor past performance, he recently was given good reason to stay on as a customer—and we suspect, it's the same reason why the bank's employees seemed newly refreshed in their jobs. Mrs. G was the new manager of the branch, and she brought to the role significant passion and enthusiasm. She tidied it up, ensured that there were tellers available at lunchtime, and would often arrange cups of coffee for her "special" customers. In short, she transformed the customer experience as well as the meaning that employees felt in their jobs by showing how each and every one of them could make a difference to performance. All the bank needed was ten thousand like her!

- British TV has a show called *The Choir* in which a gifted young conductor takes workplace groups and in a few short weeks, turns them into effective choirs. The show climaxes with a thrilling finale. One of this year's choirs was a group of firemen, and the conductor made the telling observation that while their technical musical skills needed improvement, they connected much better with the emotional import of the music than many other occupational groups—bankers, for example. The conductor's conclusion

was that the meaningful nature of their work—the fire-
fighters' focus on saving lives—put them more in tune with
their emotions.

Successful workplaces are indeed characterized by fertile connections with employees' emotional lives and personal enthusiasms. Descartes, perhaps the world's greatest rationalist philosopher,
divided the world into "mind rational" and "body irrational." And
he located the emotions in the body. He was wrong—not because
he was stupid, but because he didn't know as much about the inter-
play between brain and body, which modern neurophysiological
research has since explained. The fully rational human being is
emotional. Here is what we observed about the volunteers for the
London Olympics (first mentioned in chapter 1):

> They are all over the Games. They greet you at the air-
> port. They direct you from the trains. They guide you
> through the Olympic Park. Danny Boyle acknowledged
> them as the key to the success of the opening ceremony
> . . . their approach is a joy. They talk to strangers with
> enthusiasm. They make jokes about the weather. They are
> helpful and polite. They love what they are doing. They
> say "have a nice day" and they mean it . . . What's more,
> their enthusiasm is contagious. It affects others who
> are regular employees. Airport staff seem to have a new
> spring in their step. Policemen have a smile. The Under-
> ground staff are really keen to help you on your way. The
> people cleaning the tables at the food stalls pause to ask
> you how you are . . . If companies organized more to draw
> on and fuel enthusiasms, and less to maximize efficiency,
> the problem of disengagement would be gone forever. The
> volunteers of the Olympics hint at what an alternative
> customer experience might look like, and it looks very
> exciting.[17]

Emotions are not the froth on the cappuccino—they are the coffee. The task of the leader is to identify what is exciting about work and to convey it to others. Do this well and the energy can be infectious.

Only Connect

Organizational departments of human resources and information technology can play a really important role in building connections among the jobs people do. Indeed, one way of thinking about strategic HR is that it is in the business of cultivating cross-functional, geographically diverse connections that feed innovation and collaboration. These are the kinds of connections that enhance the meaning of work and individual jobs (thus our diagnostic statements "My duties make sense to me" and "I understand how my job fits with everyone else's").

The BBC has sometimes been very successful at juxtaposing different genres and departments to produce novel programming. The underlying theory here is that of fostering "creative collisions." Think, too, of perhaps the most fertile genre of writing in the twentieth century—science fiction, produced by a collision between the explosion of scientific writing that followed Einstein and the popular form of the novel.

Strategic IT is also in the business of enabling rich communication, often across wide geographical space. Consider Rabobank Nederland, the banking arm of the largest financial services providers in the Netherlands, Rabobank Group. After several years of development, the bank has rolled out Rabo Unplugged, an organizational and technical infrastructure that allows employees to connect to one another from practically anywhere, while still meeting the stringent encryption standard that banking systems require. With no fixed offices or rigid job descriptions, Rabobank's employees are responsible for the results of their work. But they are free to choose how, where, when, and with whom to carry it out. This approach requires managers to place an extraordinary amount of trust in subordinates, and it demands that employees become more entrepreneurial and collaborative.

But do not expect that connecting one job to another and to overall purpose will be straightforward. Old silos can prove remarkably stubborn. Even within a culture like the engineering and design company Arup the challenges can be huge. Still, Arup has long been in the business of deliberately attempting to break down the boundaries. As Arup deputy chairman Tristram Carfrae told us:

> Arup Associates has been in business for about fifty years. It's where we have architects and engineers and quantity surveyors and project managers in the same room together. They will only deploy themselves as a fully integrated team . . . it's been up and down—and it is fantastically difficult to keep on the straight and narrow, to find people who genuinely want to submerge their own egos into the collective and not have leadership in the classic sense. I found it very difficult to be there . . . as a slightly flamboyant structural engineer wrestling with when did I have the right to impose my will on the team and push it toward a structural rather than mechanical or architectural dominated solution . . . that kind of even-handed collaborative interdependence is extremely hard. Incredible rewards when it worked well and incredible frustration when it didn't.

Mind Your Social Building Blocks

Work communities vary. We may all share a desire for belonging, but what we wish to belong to can look different. We earlier distinguished between relationships of sociability and solidarity and the manner in which their interaction shapes different

communities. We regularly encourage executives to see themselves as social architects. Their responsibilities are to construct
a set of relationships that will ensure success given their varying
work contexts (our diagnostic statement "Everyone's job is necessary" reflects that implicit understanding). The social architecture
of a bank, a business school, and a boutique consulting firm are
likely to be different. This means taking account of a wide variety
of contingent factors including technology, market competition,
labor markets, environmental volatility, and national culture.

Clearly, among these various contingencies, the expectations of
employees will always play a part. What is it that they want? To
which kind of community do they wish to belong? Just as the all-en-
compassing, obsessive, almost cult-like nature of a culture like Apple
may appeal to some, it may be a nightmare to others. Remember the
business school professor who claims he goes to work to "be alone"?
The Apple obsessive might feel equally lonely in a business school.
Unilever has a rather important set of jobs for "global category managers" who are responsible for the performance of categories, like ice
cream or hair care, across the globe. They have often sought to fill
these positions by taking highly successful executives from markets
where they are doing well and offering them the chance of this
lofty head-office position. They often fail. The executives miss the
hurly-burly of the marketplace—the daily struggle against Nestle or
Procter & Gamble. Head office just seems too quiet!

Name Your Cause

If we want people to fully identify with their organizations and to
bring their best selves to work, they need a sense of cause. (This
point corresponds to our diagnostic statements "My job is meaningful to me" and "At work we share a common cause.") At Arup,
chairman Philip Dilley defines the company's cause this way:
"Take away the shareholder mantra, and you start to ask what the
firm is for . . . it's obviously for the benefit of our clients, because

without clients, you don't have a firm." Yet Dilley goes on to say that it's also for the benefit of the people working in the organization and indeed "for the benefit of the world, because we connect with our communities very strongly."

Adds Tristram Carfrae: "We are getting more and more young people who are turned on by fixing the world. It's an external focus, but it's not on the clients. It's on the planet!"

What is increasingly clear is that identifying the cause may well take you beyond the boundaries of the organization—to wider communities and perhaps the planet.

In chapters 6 and 7, we take the idea of finding meaning in organizations one step further. By avoiding stupid rules that demean people with unnecessary tasks and bureaucracy, organizations make themselves more appealing to the best workers.

Action Points for Leaders

✔ **Don't assume your motives (and your sense of what's meaningful) are shared by others.** We often know a lot about others' abilities and experience—CVs are stuffed full of this information. But how much do you know about others' motives and goals? Our experience is that for many people, this is a gap. In the absence of good information we often assume others' motives are like ours. But the overwhelming evidence is that they are not! Motives vary. It is difficult to assess what is meaningful to others without understanding their motives. Is it recognition? Or relationships? Or security? Or self-fulfillment? Or power and influence? Good leaders keep a notebook and build rich pictures of others' motives and how they may change.

✔ **Take in different experiences/get out of your comfort zone to find the meaningful.** It's hard to know how the pieces of your organization fit together and connect unless you know something about the other pieces. For example, if you are head of radio at the BBC, make sure that you are visible in TV and online. Go out of your way to connect with support staff in finance, HR, and legal. You will be amazed at how much more connected you can make your organization feel. The more connected you are, the more meaningful your work may become, as you see the link between individual effort and collective outcome.

✔ **Take every opportunity to connect your organization's efforts and outputs to the wider community.** Bring in messages from the outside. Beware organizational intro-spection. It's meaningful to know the impact you have on the wider society. Think about how many supermarkets and restaurants now take care to employ local staff and proclaim their commitment to local products.

✔ **Restate in clear, simple, and memorable ways the reason your organization exists.** What is it really for? Use stories of success and heroic failure that illustrate the answer to this question. Meaning is enhanced by a cause—and communicating it.

✔ **Build communities at work.** Whether you are in the fruit and vegetables department of a supermarket or on the executive committee of a major corporation, you have the opportunity—indeed the obligation—to build a sense of belonging and cooperation. You can do this in simple ways: by helping others willingly and by clarifying shared objectives.

Chapter 6

Simplify the Rules

Reducing the Clutter and Increasing Clarity and Fairness

W hen we were conducting the research for this book, we were impressed by the energy and passion with which people described the ideal organization. Their thinking was aspirational. They were able to articulate a positive picture of what an authentic organization should look like. The topic of this chapter is the exception. The discussion of a universal need for "simple rules" (the "S" in our DREAMS list of organizational ideals) produced waves of irritation and complaint—a kind of collective nausea. People are frustrated by what they experience as a quagmire of rules that limit their creativity and, more fundamentally, their ability to do their jobs properly. Very significantly, this frustration is shared by people outside of organizations who regularly interact with them—customers, consumers, and citizens. An abiding characteristic of modern societies is that, as individuals, we are forced to deal with increasingly faceless organizations bound by rule systems that are stunningly apathetic to our needs. This is true of people's interactions with energy companies, transport networks, telecom businesses, and the many state agencies with which we are obliged to do business.

Consider the experience of our friend Penny during a recent visit to an electronics store to have a piece of equipment repaired. Hoping to avoid frustration and waiting time, she first booked an appointment. Upon arrival (on time) at the store, she (1) was advised by the store greeter to stand in line to be "booked in." There she stood for about ten minutes before she was booked in; then she was (2) directed to wait at an available table, where she sat another ten minutes before (3) meeting with a technician. After examining the faulty equipment, the technician declared the speaker could be replaced at a cost of £45. It would take about an hour. Penny decided she would run an errand during that time, but before she could leave, she was told to (4) wait until someone came to process her order and payment. More waiting time until that step was completed, after which she (5) waited several more minutes for a receipt.

Unfortunately, when Penny returned an hour later to pick up the new piece of equipment—you guessed it—she was required to repeat steps 1 and 2 before the technician brought out the replacement. If that were the end of the story, it would be frustrating enough. Sadly, it was not the end. The next morning she discovered a different part of the new, replaced equipment was not functioning, at which point she called the store again, made another appointment, and the whole saga began again—and it continued into the following day when yet another issue forced her to return to the store! The electronics company in question? An Apple retail outlet—which illustrates how even a "sexy" company can become mired in bureaucratic processing, leaving customers feeling like a number.

As Penny told us:

> When I walked into the store and the process first started,
> it felt highly organized and all the staff seemed to be very

coordinated. But the constant waiting and being passed from one person to another just got more and more tiresome, so I ended up feeling pushed around and molded into the customer they want me to be, rather than who I am. On one level, I could totally see the rationale for their system, as I suspect the volume of customers is full-on from the moment they open to when they close. But they didn't differentiate between "cold" [walk-in] customers and those who had made appointments, and as a customer experience it certainly didn't do it for me!

This chapter is concerned with how organizations are structured to get things done, and the rules associated with that process. When thinking about how to structure labor, organizational design always comes down to two fundamental issues: division and integration. How do you divide things up, and how do you join them together? Note that there is never simply a "right" structure for organizations—they are either appropriate or inappropriate, depending on elements such as the nature of the task, the technology, the environment, and regulation. These contingencies dictate the degree of complexity in the organization, with the goal being a company that is only as complex as it needs to be and no more.

But what of organizations that don't meet that goal and instead find themselves swimming in complexity? Just how much does such inefficiency cost? Studies published in the *European Business Review* looked at the impact of complexity on companies' performance and developed a Global Simplicity Index (GSI) that correlated increased complexity with reduced profitability. Specifically: "The largest 200 companies in the Forbes Global 500 are losing, on average, 10.2 percent of their annual profits or $1.2 billion per year each due to value-destructive complexity. This adds up to an incredible collective loss of $237bn each year."[1]

Although the studies' authors acknowledge that complexity is often a necessary evil as successful firms grow and enter new markets, they see a "tipping point . . . when added complexity—a new line of products, one more acquisition, an extra layer of management—does not add proportionate value." Among the costly complexities they uncovered in organizations: changing strategy or adding strategic initiatives, convoluted hierarchies in which people report to six or more layers of management, and added complexities due to processes and systems as well as communication and coordination. The reasons *why* complexity reduces a company's profits include the fact that companies end up paying for resources and activities they don't need; they become slower and stodgier in their ability to respond to the market; and, significantly to us, because of what complexity does to *employees*—namely, it both reduces their motivation (and performance declines as complexity becomes too great) and wastes their time (leaving people distracted and exhausted by busywork). So the business case for eliminating unnecessary rules ties in nicely with our ideal organization, which attracts the best people because it keeps things simple.

Despite that research, we are not suggesting that organizations obliterate all rules. Engineers must follow procedures and tight quality controls, or buildings will collapse. Organizations need structure. Markets and enterprises need rules.

Nor are we suggesting that all rules must be formal and written down. Organizations always generate informal sets of rules, and these are at least as important as the formal ones. For example, few organizations in advanced societies today have a rule that says "women cannot be present in the top fifty officers in this company." Yet there are many companies whose informal rules make it very hard for women to reach these levels. It helps to explain why the pursuit of the diversity agenda in organizations has not been an unqualified success.

But aren't there universal characteristics that might distinguish formal rule systems that people find enabling rather than constricting? Or, to put it another way, what rules would be regarded as sensible rather than stupid? The overwhelming evidence is that generally people value:

- Fairness—the rules are applied equally to everyone.

- Clarity—the rules are as simple and clear as possible.

- Discretion—the rules allow for appropriate exercise of discretion.

- Agreement—the rules are widely shared and their purpose is clear.

- Workability—the rules can be followed and enforced.

- Authority—the rules are based on the legitimate exercise of authority.

The authentic organization keeps things simple—as far as possible. It develops rules that allow systematization without bureaucratization. Our distinction between these two phenomena is clear. When organizations systematize, people know what the rules are for; when they bureaucratize, the rules seems to have no function. These rules, in effect, become the conditions for freedom. They protect what is good in the organization rather than undermine it. Chairman David Evans at London's House of St Barnabas put it to us this way:

> The difference is trust. If you don't trust people, you get lots of rules. We stress trust when we hire and try to reinforce it in all our daily practices. But it can occasionally go wrong and you get let down. You just have to accept that— if you revert back straightaway to rules, you've had it. You need to allow people to experiment within a framework.

What we are talking about in this chapter is no less than the three big themes that are key to well-functioning societies as well as organizations: freedom, fairness, and authority (which are a distillation of the six values in the preceding bulleted list). Later in the chapter our diagnostic will help you determine how your organization rates when it comes to having simple rules, and we will suggest ways for developing rules that foster creativity and innovation, attract talent, and allow people to do their jobs as well as they possibly can.

Let's begin by examining one of the themes, authority, because it is central to a key question: Where do rules come from, and are they perceived as legitimate?

Authority

The people we spoke to in our fieldwork were looking for legitimacy in organizational rules.

Although it is true that organizational hierarchies have flattened in recent years, organizations nevertheless remain what sociologist Max Weber calls "imperatively coordinated associations." That is to say, they are fundamentally structures of power and authority. Weber defines authority as the legitimate exercise of power.

He distinguishes among three forms of authority. The first rests on the social characteristics of groups of individuals—for example, age, which might give us a gerontocracy, or gender, which might give rise to patriarchy or matriarchy. He calls this "traditional authority." The second he calls "charismatic authority," which rests on the peculiar characteristics of the individual. One of his key examples here is Jesus Christ, whom he describes as a charismatic leader. Curiously, in modern business organizations we have become rather obsessed with this form of authority. The final form Weber calls "rational legal authority," which rests upon the carefully defined roles and responsibilities of the officeholder.

One of the key themes of Weber's work is that modern societies are increasingly dominated by this rational form of authority, in particular through the development of bureaucracies. In modern parlance, we are apt to describe bureaucracies as slow and inefficient. But for Weber their proliferation is to be understood rather through their efficiency, their ability to reduce the complex reality of human individuality to types and processes. This view leads him to the rather gloomy conclusion that the modern world is doomed to progressive rationalization—"the disenchantment of the world."

The pessimism of Weber has been echoed in modern culture. Balzac describes bureaucracies as "the giant power wielded by pygmies." The novels of Franz Kafka can also be interpreted as tragic stories of individuals trapped in bureaucratic structures they cannot comprehend. You are on trial but you do not know what for (*The Trial*). You seek to enter an institution but you don't know how to get in (*The Castle*). A more modern, and at least superficially more humorous, expression of this sentiment can be found in Joseph Heller's *Catch 22*.

Despite all of this grim pessimism, in our view, organizations don't have to be like this—they can rest upon legitimate bases of authority. Indeed, we go further by suggesting another form of authority—moral authority based on the legitimacy of ends and not on the efficiency of means. For example, the aspiration of design-firm founder Ove Arup was to promote a "humanitarian" attitude that creates an organization that is "human and friendly in spite of being large and efficient. Where every member is treated not only as a link in a chain of command, not only as a wheel in a bureaucratic machine, but as a human being whose happiness is the concern of all, who is treated not only as a means but as an end."[2]

Arup's underlying philosophy is that good people will be attracted by interesting work—the opportunity for creativity and personal growth. If someone becomes "frustrated by red tape or by having someone breathing down his neck," Arup continues, "someone for whom he has scant respect, if he has little influence on decisions which affect his work, and which he may not agree with, then he will pack up and go. And so he should. It is up to us, therefore, to create an organization which will allow gifted individuals to unfold." We can derive several illuminating insights from this inspirational speech. The first is its insistence on "humanity"—where individuals are treated as ends, not means. For surely Weber was correct when he pointed out the potentially dehumanizing consequences of bureaucratization. The second is its insistence on the unnecessary constraining consequences of "red tape"—a theme we will return to in a moment. Finally, it captures well the notion that we should never blindly follow those in power. We have a moral duty to examine the bases of their authority. There are moral imperatives for followers just as there are for leaders.

Freedom

When we were collecting data for this book, one of the most impassioned pleas from respondents was that they desired the exercise of freedom at work. It was not the absence of rules that they wanted, however. They required clarity, agreement, and the possibility of discretion—not some form of organizational anarchism. It was almost as if they shared Spinoza's somewhat cryptic definition of freedom as "knowledge of necessity." That is to say, they recognized the function of some rules and the stultifying effects of others.

As we have pointed out elsewhere, the engineering and design company Arup is founded upon the guiding idea of looking for "good people" and then giving them significant scope to express their talents. Arup has worked hard to protect freedoms and to resist the temptation to excessively formalize its approach to management.

A more recent example is streaming-media company Netflix, established in 1997. It has worked hard at retaining this sense of freedom for its employees despite its prodigious growth. Its approach to human resource management rests upon the assumption that if you hire people who put the company's interests first and who understand the company DNA, then they will "do the right thing." Netflix deliberately avoids spending time and money on writing and enforcing HR policies that, in the company's view, are simply unnecessary for most of the staff. Salaried employees, for example, are free to decide how much time they will take for holiday leave. Bosses and workers work it out with each other. Simple guidelines are provided—in accounting and finance, for example, it's not OK to be away during the busy end of quarter periods. Or if you take thirty days consecutively, you will need to meet with HR. There is a similar approach with travel and expenses policy. It's best summed up in five simple words: "Act in Netflix's best interests." The expectation is that people will spend company money as if it were their own.

Broadly speaking, it seems as if they do. Expect responsible behavior, and most employees will comply. Formal performance reviews are also eliminated. Instead, Netflix employees are encouraged to have regular conversations about their performance. There is an explicit recognition of the dangers of formal performance reviews, which may become ritualistic, political, and dishonest. This is not to say that feedback on performance is ignored. Netflix conducts regular 360-degree reviews, but these are kept informal and simple. People are just asked to identify what colleagues should stop, start, or continue. Again, this kind of honesty and freedom seems to deliver results.[3]

In another company and industry, consider the words of Zhang Ruimin, CEO of highly successful Chinese company Haier:

> Today, I believe, what Haier's employees need is to be allowed to make decisions for themselves and not to feel that they are following me in their work. The philosopher Lao-tzu said, "In the highest antiquity, the people did not know that there were rulers." I take his meaning to be that a leader whose existence is unknown to his subordinates is really the most brilliant one.[4]

In stark contrast, many organizations are characterized by an insidious form of "rule creep," a seemingly never-ending accretion until people experience a kind of miasma of rules. Some organizations have so many rules that it is almost impossible not to be in breach of some of them at any given time and maybe not even be aware!

To understand this process, we return to the classic sociological analysis of Alvin W. Gouldner in his groundbreaking book *Patterns of Industrial Bureaucracy.*[5] Gouldner studied a gypsum manufacturing plant in the early 1950s and used this to test and extend Max Weber's seminal work on the rise of the bureaucracy. Gouldner distinguishes among three kinds of rules.

First, there are punishment-centered rules. For example, if your expenses claims are dishonest you will be disciplined, even fired; or if you are regularly late for work you will be sanctioned. Gouldner insightfully recognizes that these rules can work in two directions. When exercised by management we might call them the "disciplinary procedure"; when exercised by workers they take the form of "collective grievance." Most significantly, both parties see the rules as imposed.

Second, Gouldner describes representative rules. These rules are viewed by everyone as their own. For example, in the gypsum plant both management and union initiated and developed a safety program. Both sides saw it as in their interests to promote safety. For management, such safety regulations ensured continuous production; for the union, the rules reflected the high value placed on personal and bodily welfare.

Finally, Gouldner describes "mock rules." These rules take two forms. An example of the first is the no-smoking rule in the gypsum plant. Because this rule was imposed by the insurance company, neither workers nor management take it seriously and it is widely broken. The second form is rather more pernicious. These rules gain their power from the possibility that they may be either applied or ignored. Think about any random workplace and a rule that says, "You are not allowed to take your laptops home." For the powerful, that is to say the rule enforcers, they have the choice to either apply the rule or to selectively ignore it. As in, "You've done a good job this week, so you can take your laptop home." These latter rules can give rise to an indulgency pattern where some employees are perceived as favorites for whom the rules are often waived. This is where a vicious circle of rule accretion begins because—guess what—to cure the indulgency pattern, the organization develops a new set of rules.

Gouldner's analysis raises some fundamental questions about the nature of rules in organizations. What is their purpose? Whose interests do they serve? Are they clear (to encourage agreement) or opaque (to encourage the rise of indulgency patterns)? These questions become particularly important, for example, in successful entrepreneurial businesses. As they grow, the founder-owners often come to believe that new, complicated processes and rules will undermine their culture. But systemization need not lead to bureaucratization—not if people understand what the rules are for and view them as legitimate.

Vestergaard Frandsen, a start-up social enterprise that makes mosquito netting for the developing world, has worked hard at this. The company is mastering the art of behavior codes that can help structure its growing operations without jeopardizing its culture. Hiring (and firing) decisions are intentionally simple—only one level of approval is required for each position. Regional directors have significant freedom within clear deadlines and top and bottom-line targets. Knowledge-management systems are designed to encourage people to phone rather than e-mail one another and to explain why someone is being cc'ed on an e-mail message. Vestergaard sees these simple rules as safeguards rather than threats to its founding values.

A similar example comes from Medicover, a private health care company founded in 1995 that operates in central and eastern Europe. This fast-growing business has 10,500 employees (mainly medical professionals and skilled technicians) across twelve countries. Its main market is Poland where, with health-service privatization imminent, the market is likely to grow explosively. But Medicover faces severe competition, mainly from venture capital–funded companies. That is why CEO Fredrik Ragmark has deliberately attempted to distinguish the company's culture from, in his words, "the very different kind of organizational behavior which operates amongst our competitors."

To attract and keep the limited supply of talented professional employees, Ragmark took a two-pronged approach. First, in 1997 he established the Medicover Foundation through which the company supports a range of pro bono projects; this was joined in 2011 by another charitable foundation (set up with a donation from Medicover's majority owner) that allows Medicover to address wider health issues, such as diabetes, within the communities in which it operates. In these pro bono activities, employees are free to find ways in which they can help. Second, Ragmark has deliberately developed a culture of what he calls "operational freedom." Although this involves hiring people that naturally fit in at Medicover, it does not mean mindless conformity. In selection interviewing, for example, colleagues are encouraged to look for what Ragmark calls "authentic human differences," and to subsequently urge new hires to keep those differences alive at work (which aligns nicely with the first of our DREAMS chapters, on seeking out and nurturing people's differences). But there is also a recognition that with organizational growth comes the need for new kinds of parameters. For example, employees in control functions such as finance and accounting are encouraged to act in a collaborative fashion, and all employees are encouraged to protect the Medicover founding values.

These are positive examples of organizations developing appropriate systems without unnecessary bureaucracy. But there are many examples of companies that fail.

Even iconic cultures of innovation can slip up. HP has developed a prodigious reputation as a culture that encourages innovation by abolishing rigid chains of command, rejecting elaborate executive offices, and putting employees on first-name terms, among other initiatives. But even in its heyday in the late 1980s, HP was becoming bogged down in bureaucratic rituals. *Business Week* reported that one general manager was dealing with no fewer than thirty-eight in-house committees. Establishing a name for the company's NewWave Computing software took nearly seven months and a hundred people in nine committees. More generally, a complex web of committees designed to improve communication between disparate operating groups only served to push up costs and slow down development. In attempting to move into "open systems," a series of committees was established to select appropriate technologies and products. But here, too, committees "kept multiplying like a virus." According to one analyst: "Everything was by committee . . . no one could make a decision."[6]

In authentic organizations, individuals have clarity about the rules, about which they generally agree. They also have discretion to deal with unique situations, while recognizing that the expression of freedom within organizations rests on a necessary degree of constraint.

This seems like a straightforward series of demands. Yet the enemy—ever-increasing bureaucratization—remains with us. We do not share Max Weber's grim predictions for mankind "trapped in an iron cage of his own making . . . from which he cannot escape." But it would be naive to imagine that it's a simple task to establish rules that encourage innovation, creativity, and discretion.

Fairness

Finally, when people describe the dream organization, they ask for rules to be fair. There are libraries of research on fairness at work, but here we focus on two particular meanings. The first we have already described: people desire rules whose purpose is clear and with which they generally agree. The second is that they want the rules to apply equally to everyone. The Occupy Wall Street (OWS) movement that began in New York in September 2011 and spread across the country offered a very public reflection of this sentiment. With an underlying focus on income inequality in the United States and financial greed and corruption, OWS demanded that the rules governing things such as corporate fraud and rate fixing be applied equally across all institutions. Especially in light of the global financial crisis that became apparent in 2007–2008, the widespread public view has been that none of the big corporate players were held to account.

Note that when it comes to applying rules equally to everyone, there are some important caveats. Clearly, cultural variations abound in definitions of fairness. The American sociologist Talcott Parsons drew a distinction between universalistic and particularistic societies.[7] In the former, the rules apply equally to everyone. In the latter, it is more acceptable that rules are applied differentially. For example, many contemporary Latin cultures remain significantly particularistic. And particularism is certainly a feature of the modern Middle East. Those realities notwithstanding, in a globalized and connected world all institutions are increasingly judged by universalistic standards. The unfolding drama of the Arab Spring bears stark testimony to this trend.

Turning our focus to organizations, what characterizes rules that apply to everyone? We can derive some important clues from distinctive organizational cultures. And because, as is often observed, cultures are primarily oral, when analyzing organizational culture we are interested in the *stories* that organizations tell about themselves.[8]

So think like an anthropologist as we recount two stories about a very famous British retailer—for many years regarded as the most successful in Europe. The first involves a rather gifted marketer. Sadly, he has something of a drink problem. One day he arrives at his office at ten in the morning after a late night of carousing. As he enters the elevator he is followed by the company chairman, who remarks sharply, "Late again?" The clever marketer replies, "Funny, so am I!"

Here is the second story. That same marketer is based in the department that monitors the sales of new product lines across the business. It has become something of an organizational ritual that at the end of the day, the chairman visits the new-lines department to check on sales. On this occasion, the chairman has to leave a little early. So he visits the new-lines office and asks the marketer to report on sales, which he duly does in some detail. Later that evening the chairman, who has by now become a little absent-minded, thinks that he has forgotten to check on the new-line sales so he arrives at the office early the next morning to do so. For once, the clever marketer is there on time. The chairman asks him to report on the sales of new lines. After some deliberation, he replies sincerely, "All stores report a quiet night."

So what do these two stories tell us about the culture of this organization and the structure of the rules? The first tells us that the rules apply equally to everyone—if the marketer is late then so too is the chairman. The second tells us that if you receive an instruction from a senior manager, then you act on it.

The stories come from Marks and Spencer some years ago. The culture of the British department store, founded as a market stall by two Jewish migrants in Leeds, is reminiscent of a Jewish family.

It is characterized by a rule system that applies equally to everyone and where there are high levels of respect for authority figures. The rules are perceived as fair, because they have a purpose, and are applied universally. Authority relationships are seen as legitimate. The chairman has a right to ask about the new lines just as Jewish parents have a right to ask that you be home for Shabbat.

More recently, another venerable British institution (and a global brand)—the BBC—has been rocked by a series of scandals that reflect informal rules that were applied in decidedly unfair and harmful ways. The first involves extremely serious allegations about sexual assaults against children perpetrated by Jimmy Savile, a former leading light of BBC entertainment. The scandal is shocking in its scale and depravity. But what has rocked the BBC is the extent to which its own procedures and rules were apparently ignored for its stars. More shocking still, it seems the same is true for some of the hospitals where Savile was a volunteer.

In the same organization, serious questions have been asked about severance payments to senior executives. The former director general, Mark Thompson (now president and CEO of the *New York Times*), and other colleagues were asked to give evidence before the UK's Public Accounts Committee. It appears that excessive payments were made, well beyond contractual obligations, to several senior executives. When questioned about these, HR director Lucy Adams attempted to explain them not by reference to any measure of merit or fairness but by saying she was simply following "custom and practice." Adams resigned under a cloud shortly afterward. A member of the Public Accounts Committee said that senior executives had "presided over" a culture of "corporate fraud and cronyism."[9]

What Organizations Can Do

Now that we have looked at examples of how rules often function in organizations, let's explore specific ways to ensure rules that are both fair and simple. The sidebar "Does Your Organization

Diagnostic: Does Your Organization Have Simple, Agreed-On Rules?

1 = Strongly Disagree   2 = Disagree   3 = Neither Agree Nor Disagree
4 = Agree   5 = Strongly Agree

_____ We keep things simple.

_____ The rules are clear and apply equally to everyone.

_____ I know what the rules are for.

_____ Everyone knows what the rules are for.

_____ We, as an organization, resist unnecessary rules and paperwork.

_____ Authority is respected.

Consider any statement to which you assign a 1 or 2 as worth your sustained attention. An overall score below 18 suggests that this area of your organizational life requires improvement. Ask yourself how long you will give the organization to make genuine progress.

Have Simple, Agreed-On Rules?" contains a portion of the diagnostic we use in our work with organizations to identify how their internal rules function.

The responses to these questions from senior executives are the most negative of all. And of the items in the diagnostic, the lowest scoring is "We, as an organization, resist unnecessary rules and paperwork." While executives score a little more positively on "I know what the rules are for," their views are not widely shared by others in the organization. In addition, lower-level participants are convinced that the rules are not applied equally to everyone. It is not surprising, therefore, that fairness is a major issue.

We can draw from the diagnostic statements themselves some core essential dynamics operating in organizations that maintain simple rules. These suggest four organizational imperatives in particular that we garnered from our research.

Simplify, Simplify

The diagnostic statements "We keep things simple" and "We, as an organization, resist unnecessary rules and paperwork" mirror an imperative to prevent the ever-present danger of rule creep, which means that organizations need to continuously check where they stand on this goal. Remember HP and how it suddenly found itself mired in committee overload.

Being mindful about keeping things simple in the corporate culture is of utmost importance to Jess Lee, CEO of the fashion website Polyvore. She says, "We have three values. The first one is 'delight the user.' The others are 'do a few things well' and 'make an impact' . . . We believe that you have to keep things as simple as possible, edit out the things that are unnecessary or extraneous, and focus on polishing the details." She makes sure that both the user experience and the processes within the company reflect those priorities. One month last year, for example, she declared a "simplification month." "We just asked everyone in the company to make a list of everything they do, identify the things that are important, and for the rest of the list, simplify it, optimize it, or delete it so we can get the company to the simplest possible state." Streamlining on a regular basis remains a top priority. "It's really important to take the time to clean up all the entropy that otherwise will happen," Lee says.[10]

Organizations of all types and sizes can be vulnerable to creeping bureaucracy. A leading global business school we know well employs around 450 people—about a hundred of whom are academics. We discussed our research with the dean and asked him to consider where the school ranked on the various dimensions of the dream organization. He identified the need for simple, agreed-upon rules as the greatest challenge.

Perhaps academics—like many specialized professions—revel in complexity! As with many universities, there is a matrix structure that interfaces programs with faculty departments. The resulting scope for committees and debate is large indeed. Or take, for example, the rules that surround tenure processes. At their worst, these can be byzantine and give huge opportunity for different interpretation and debate. Strict adherence to a simple rule of "five publications in the top six A-grade journals within seven years from hire" is one way forward. But first you need agreement about which six journals—and why. And then you need to deal with the different rankings of the four external assessors working in different business schools with divergent views on the best journals. At this point you have not even begun the discussion about which of the candidate's publications actually have influence. Where are they cited? And which citation indices are the most reliable? Similar dramas surround assessment processes in professional service firms when consideration is given to partnership status, for example. It requires constant vigilance to keep the process away from damaging rule proliferation and complexity.

Don't Attempt Tick-Box "Fairness"

This imperative follows from the statement in our diagnostic: "The rules are clear and apply equally to everyone." But do not look to a rules-based system to enforce fairness and equality, because it will probably fail. That is not to say that a legal organizational charter or document that defines rights and responsibilities isn't useful. It's more that this is a necessary but insufficient condition for fairness at work. Fairness arises from shared values and agreed-upon rules—other elaborate rule-based interventions may collapse into a tick-box charade.

Take CEO Navin Nagiah of DNN, a web-content software company. The culture he's trying to foster is one that is "very open, honest, and direct." Yet he recognizes that while honesty and fairness about factual issues is relatively straightforward, not everything can be easily legislated: "The harder part to inculcate is intellectual honesty." He offers an example of a team member opposing an idea in a meeting. If the intent is not to make the idea better, but rather to push forward another agenda, "that's intellectual dishonesty and that leads to a bad culture." What matters at DNN is "whether you're authentic, whether you really want [your colleagues] to do well, that you want the organization to do well, and that you are committed."[11] In our view, these are issues of fairness that are critical in organizations—and none of these things can be enforced through sets of corporate rules.

Remember What the Rules Are For

Connecting rules to goals and to purpose is vital (thus our diagnostic statements "I know what the rules are for" and "Everyone knows what the rules are for"). There is a mountain of depressing evidence to show that even members of relatively small-scale teams can forget what their goals and objectives are. They are more likely to remember them if they are regularly revisited and, if necessary, refreshed. More widely, it is a challenge to connect individual and team tasks to an overall organizational purpose. We visited this theme in our earlier chapters on meaning at work and authenticity. Good rules connect to purpose.

An executive vice president we know of who heads sales operations and marketing at a privately held midsize US company highlighted this point for us: "There was a step in our processes that was creating undue hardship for the sales team. But I didn't even know the step existed! When one of my reps pointed out the problem to me, I was really grateful and we streamlined the whole thing right away." That story is a testament both to this manager's ability to keep an open channel of communication with her staff and to the benefits of regularly reviewing rules and systems that are in place.

Think: Where Does Authority Come From?

The ideal organization gives you deeply motivating reasons to submit to the structures that support the company's overarching purpose. We can see the importance of such authority by observing the trouble that emerges in its absence (thus our diagnostic statement "Authority is respected"). For example, we have noted a common problem among the major pharmaceutical companies we've worked with over the years, places like Roche, Novartis, GlaxoSmithKline, and Johnson & Johnson: How do you develop successful leaders in an R&D environment? Research organizations have hundreds of very clever people who are interested in their research obsessions—cures for complex cancers, forms of dementia, diabetes. But they are often utterly *un*interested in the indispensible task of effectively administering the organization or taking a leadership role in it. There are also some—usually people in support functions like finance or HR—who have a deep interest in the effective operation of the organization. Unfortunately, they absolutely lack legitimacy with the research scientists, who perceive them as bureaucratic obstacles to their "breakthrough research." But there are a few—very few—research scientists who come to see that through the exercise of legitimate authority and the practice of leadership, they can become even better at drug development. These people are like gold dust and can make the difference between an average pharmaceutical company and a great one.

Somewhat curiously, there are parallels in the music industry. There are executives who love hanging around with artists and who enjoy the cool lifestyle. The problem is they can't read a contract or write a marketing plan. There are others who are as commercially sharp as razors; they can read and dissect a contract at a hundred yards. The problem here is that they have no affinity with the artists—and the feeling is reciprocated! And then there are the very few who are respected by the artists and who possess considerable commercial acumen. They have legitimate authority—and around it you can build great record companies.

This discussion of simple rules concludes the six dimensions of authentic organizations. Taken together, they constitute a challenging agenda for all kinds of organizations. And we are not naive enough to think that all of them can be easily achieved. In the next chapter, we explore the tensions among the dimensions and the trade-offs that people and organizations must make. We will also help you to think about where to start and which of the dimensions are the biggest priorities for your organization.

Action Points for Leaders

✔ **When things go wrong, resist the temptation to invent another rule.** Where you can, try trust first, and accept that this may not always produce what you want. Rules may look like a quick fix, but they can inspire a "low trust" downward spiral that typically creates more problems.

✔ **Don't ask others to do things that you wouldn't do yourself.** You are unlikely to engender respect for the rules—or for yourself—if you repeatedly create exceptions for yourself or for others. If you have rules, believe in them!

✔ **Check how the rules affect all stakeholders.** Rules affect not just employees and regulators, but also customers and the wider society. Next time you introduce a new rule, be sure to examine the impact it might have on customers, consumers, suppliers, and other stakeholders.

✔ **Organizations should be as complex as they need to be—but not more.** Some businesses, like innovative pharmaceutical companies, are intrinsically complex. The people who get to the top of organizations often get there because they are good at complexity. But paradoxically, once they get there, they must strive for simplicity.

✔ **Explain the purpose of the rules.** People are much more likely to follow them when they understand their raison d'être.

✔ **Be prepared to reexamine your underlying business processes.** By looking carefully at the details that constitute every way your organization does business, you can eliminate unnecessary complexity.

Chapter 7

Creating and Sustaining the Authentic Organization

Trade-Offs and Challenges

I t would be unrealistic to expect any single organization to excel in everything, but some companies are showing the way on particular dimensions, as we've seen throughout this book. These are the companies that provide the *inspiration* to turn *aspiration* into reality.

In this chapter, we look at the typical choices and challenges organizations must confront to make themselves into places where people want to work. Clearly, the DREAMS elements we've been describing connect to one another. You are likely to better acknowledge difference if you are honest; if you are honest, you will be more authentic; and if you are free of needless bureaucratic controls, your work will be more meaningful.

But they are also in tension, both with each other and with forces outside the organization. For example, financial services and pharmaceutical companies have to come to terms with more intrusive, penetrating, and complex regulation. In such an environment, producing a culture of simple rules is an enormous challenge. Radical honesty may be a challenge when your key competitive advantage is tied to intellectual property.

It is also true that being very strong on one dimension does not necessarily predict strength elsewhere. Enron was widely celebrated as an exemplary organization for its "simple rules."[1] It was not until the lights started to go off in California that we knew something was seriously wrong. And as we have shown in this book, the design firm Arup gains strength from its celebration of difference and individual expression. But the cost comes in lengthy and complex decision-making processes that might benefit from some simple rules. Tine is a successful Norwegian food cooperative with a healthy Nordic belief in fairness. However, its insistence on wide and deep consultation slows decision making and hinders innovation. Denmark's Novo Nordisk, one of the top ten largest global pharma companies, gives us lessons in the practice of radical honesty but constantly struggles with issues around difference because its employees are primarily Danish, as is the company worldview.

As we explore in this chapter the dilemmas and trade-offs that companies will likely confront, we show that an appreciation of existing organizational context and history is important. So too is where you start: Which element of the dream organization should attention be focused on—and why? And who should be paying attention? Although differing elements may call upon different areas of functional expertise, it seems unlikely that the authentic organization will be created or sustained without the full attention of top management.

Who Do You Think You Are?

So what kind of organization are you? Before thinking of change, conduct a thorough diagnosis of your current position. Our research illustrates a variety of contexts and organizational types.

Compare, for example, the "blank page" context of the small high-tech or creative agency start-up with that of established organizations with long and distinctive histories, such as Heineken, Unilever, or IBM. Think, too, of the contrast between these "conventional" capitalist enterprises and those that have alternative ownership structures and/or distinctive ideals—for example, Arup, Novo Nordisk, New York Life, John Lewis (an employee-based partnership), and Vestergaard Frandsen (a private enterprise with a social purpose).

Finally, consider organizations such as Apple, Google, Starbucks, Amazon, Facebook, or Cisco, all relatively young businesses that have experienced explosive growth, created global brands, and have huge capital value. Today, as "established" businesses, they have become characterized by conventional ownership structures, although they clearly started with "alternative" ideals—to make information freely available, to let people "be themselves," to "do no evil." So we might well ask ourselves: Are these companies modern exemplars of the dream—transparent, tolerating difference and personal freedom, and providing moral purpose? Or are some of them showing signs of old problems—secrecy rather than transparency, conformity rather than diversity, and a profit imperative that results in "immoral" Third World wages and sophisticated corporate-tax-evasion schemes? Frederick Taylor would surely recognize (and probably applaud) the routines, processes, and measures experienced by those who work in the vast Amazon warehouses.

To be sure, as we pointed out in chapter 3, the San Francisco Bay area—that once wildly diverse and creative hub of tech companies like Apple and Google—seems to have morphed in recent years into an expanded Silicon Valley, with its growing tech-elitist population of well-educated, primarily white males. The following newspaper excerpt describes how San Francisco ultimately may be undermined by these changes, and it features an interview with the ninety-four-year-old poet and painter Lawrence Ferlinghetti. An early champion of Beat poets Allen Ginsberg and Jack Kerouac and co-owner of the renowned City Lights bookshop and publisher, Ferlinghetti came to San Francisco in 1951 because he heard it was a great place to be a bohemian. But today he doesn't feel so at home in the city. Although he still lives in his North Beach working-class Italian neighborhood, the once-affordable rents and European atmosphere have all but disappeared.

> [Ferlinghetti] complains of a "soulless group of people," a "new breed" of men and women too busy with iPhones to "be here" in the moment, and shiny new Mercedes-Benzes on his street. The major art galley in central San Francisco that has shown Ferlinghetti's work for two decades is closing because it can't afford the new rent. It, along with several other galleries, will make way for a cloud computing startup called MuleSoft said to have offered to triple the rent. "It is totally shocking to see Silicon Valley take over the city," says Ferlinghetti. "San Francisco is radically changing and we don't know where it is going to end up."[2]

The image of San Francisco as a city melding with the tech companies and workers it hosts into some kind of "soulless" soup should give us all pause. At the very least it should prompt serious self-examination on the part of organizations. Ask yourself whether your organization is truly the kind of place that you think (or hope) it is. Is it as diverse and creative as you think?

This is a key question when looking at where your organization is now and where it hopes to be in terms of becoming the kind of place that will attract and retain the best people.

All of the differing contexts we're describing here suggest distinctive challenges in *creating, sustaining,* or *recapturing* the dream organization. Let's begin with a look at a gaming company, Supercell, which in a rather deliberate way is in the midst of creating just such a place—and confronting the dilemmas inherent in the process.

Dream Weaving

We were introduced to Supercell by David Gardner, one of its investors and an old friend of ours whom we first met when he was boss of Electronic Arts (EA) in Europe. Supercell is an impressive Finnish start-up that dominates the sector of games made for tablets and smartphones, based on just a few very successful offerings. In 2014, its "Clash of Clans" was the top-grossing iPad game in 122 countries worldwide, and another Supercell game, "Hay Day," tops the lists in 78 countries. Its most recent release, "Boom Beach," looks set to be another success.

Although Gardner is an investor, in the company presentations you will hear clearly that "we are *not* EA." One of the team, Tibor Tóth, remarks, "There are no mantras on the walls here, no big words on company culture." Supercell celebrates the fact that "people come from a diverse set of backgrounds personally and professionally"—and that "we know where we come from . . . we're humble." How, then, do they see themselves? Not as rock stars but as "creative craftsmen."[3]

Supercell has built its organization around small teams with no more than half a dozen employees in each team so that there is "no hierarchy or bureaucracy." What distinguishes these teams? Their goal is to put together "insanely" talented individuals, give them "unrestricted freedom," and at the same time build a "great team chemistry."

Gardner says that although the gaming industry has become very "indie," with most start-ups focusing on creativity and an "almost total lack of interest in making money," this is not what the founders of Supercell are doing. They want success for themselves and their employees too, Gardner says. Accordingly, Supercell has developed a financial model that works—*very* well. While most of what Supercell produces is free (90 percent of users pay nothing), significant revenues come from the 10 percent who buy a more sophisticated gaming experience. The result: its business of only 160 employees brings in between \$1.5 billion and 2 billion euros annually! (EA by comparison has seven thousand people and lower revenues.)

One key to Supercell's success has been the way it builds relationships with users to eventually convert them to the 10 percent. The company does this by carefully listening to and respecting customers, creating "clans" (communities) who want to play its games. But the company also makes sure it listens to employees. When it came time to articulate what the company stood for, cofounder and CEO Ilkka Paananen sat down with every one of Supercell's fifty-five employees at the time for a chat. He asked why they liked it there, and what they didn't like. In other words, he was asking them, Why should anyone work here? This formed the basis of the company's values (see the sidebar "Supercell Spells Out 'What We Believe'").

Here, then, is a start-up with a mission! Supercell's founders have a crystal clear idea of what they want to be—and what they *don't* want to be (EA!). Look at their ambitions, beliefs, and values, and you will see a company that seems, more than most, to have aspirations on every one of the six dimensions of the dream organization.

This exemplary clarity and strength of purpose distinguishes Supercell. It provides wonderful lessons for those who have the opportunity to *create* from scratch. But the question remains: Can these ideals be sustained?

Supercell Spells Out "What We Believe"

Small is beautiful—With the right people and team chemistry, we believe small teams can produce the best games and the biggest results.

Full transparency—All of our numbers, data, and plans about the business—good and bad—are shared with everyone. The free flow of information improves communication, decision making, trust, and morale.

Zero bureaucracy—Our small, independent teams are nimble and move very fast, so it's important to remove any obstacles that might get in their way and slow them down.

Extreme independence—Small teams alone aren't enough. Those teams must have the freedom to make quick decisions and take risks.

Pride in craft—Although our teams move fast, we try hard never to compromise on creativity or quality. Our players generously share their precious time with us and we want to return the favor by giving them deliriously fun game experiences.

Take care of our own—Top pay, industry-leading benefits, work–life balance, and a commitment to the whole human being is the secret to happy, high-performing people. And that's our commitment.

Source: "Our Story," Supercell company website, www.supercell.com/en/our-story/.

Keep the Dream Alive

The evidence from previous start-ups of various types suggests that Supercell will face some familiar traps, such as:

- **Loss of founders' energy.** Those who start businesses are inspired by creating something new; they can become bored once the initial challenges are overcome and an operating organization must be managed. They can become disillusioned with the quality of their potential successors.

- **Loss of focus with growth.** Increasing scale is often accompanied by a diversification of activity that takes the business away from its original obsessions. Should Supercell go into amusement parks or films? The offers are there but the dangers of diluting the company's identity are real. Supercell's CEO sees protecting the culture and attracting great people as his major challenge—and if it means saying no to growth opportunities, he is prepared to do it.

- **Difficulty in retaining small, independent teams with scale.** The attractions of sharing experience, expertise, and resources across a growing organization are obvious—if only to avoid reinventing the wheel. But as interdependencies increase, local team autonomy is threatened.

- **Confusion of systems with bureaucracy.** As we showed in chapter 6, organizations need rules, but these can proliferate in ways that make it difficult to remember what the rules are for and how they contribute to purpose; original freedoms become compromised.

One big challenge that Supercell founders already know they face going forward: the need to expand beyond Helsinki (even though 40 percent of its employees are non-Finn technicians who have been brought into Helsinki). As of now, the organization's expansion is driven by a very narrow talent pool, so it has opened offices in San Francisco, Seoul, and Tokyo in hopes of widening its employee base. But how will Supercell transport its culture beyond Finland? And there is also the question of how far it will want to go in decentralizing its operations. As founding CEO Ilkka Paananen is very well aware, the challenges of growing while maintaining effective communication—even if only between four offices—can become profound.

Meantime, what challenges do other organizations face when it comes to sustaining the dream? Some companies seem to have been successful in retaining their early founding magic. There are lessons here from several of the larger, established organizations we have discussed in this book. The strengths of organizations such as New York Life, Johnson & Johnson, Heineken, BMW, and Arup revolves—to a significant degree—around their clarity of purpose, acknowledgment of heritage, and obsessional attention to the practice of core values. In effect, much of what we explored in our discussion of authenticity (chapter 4) sheds light on what might be needed to sustain early dreams.

But success can also be achieved by working on other fronts. Remember, for example, Novo Nordisk's diligent application of organizational audits to facilitate open and honest exchange of information. Or think of the explicit efforts made by Arup to resist bureaucracy and to continue to find places for difference. Finally, don't forget the creative initiatives of EY's UK office, whose charity ThinkForward offers opportunities for staff to make a social contribution in their communities, thereby fostering novel, value-adding opportunities and sources of meaning for talented professionals.

Rekindling the Dream

Organizations that once were known as "dream" places to work, but now find themselves trying to recapture those golden days, face a very different set of issues from companies trying to create or sustain the dream. Toward the end of our research, we began to work with one of the world's major global banks—Barclays. Like most of the major financial players, it had been hugely affected by the financial crash of 2008. It did manage to avoid a major state bail-out and to acquire large chunks of Lehman Brothers, but subsequent events mired it in a series of scandals involving the fixing of the LIBOR rate and the questionable selling of financial products. Its reputational capital was severely damaged. The swashbuckling CEO, Bob Diamond, once the darling of investment bankers, left the bank, as did many of his acolytes.

He was replaced by Antony Jenkins, a man who could not have been more *unlike* Bob Diamond. Quiet and relatively unassuming, Jenkins had a career that included both the retail and credit card sectors. Yet he has launched one of the most ambitious projects in the history of financial services, called the Transform project. Its intention is to reinvent Barclays and, as he often makes clear, this will involve reinventing banking. You may think that it's hard to reinvent banking without reinventing capitalism! So you can see it's a pretty big project.

Although it's too early to tell whether the changes will work (as we write, the bank is about two years into the process), Barclays has energy and ambition. Many of its themes are connected to the arguments we have made in this book; in particular, Transform seeks to embrace the principles of radical honesty as the bank attempts to rebuild its reputational capital so damaged by successive financial scandals. In addition, Barclays has invested heavily in exploring the implications of authenticity both for its own leaders and for its relationship with its customers. Jenkins has tried to reconnect with the Quaker origins of Barclays and to build a bank with a strong ethical foundation. Thus, the five values of Transform are as follows:

- **Respect:** We respect and value those we work with, and the contribution that they make.

- **Integrity:** We act fairly, ethically and openly in all we do.

- **Service:** We put our clients and customers at the centre of what we do.

- **Excellence:** We use our energy, skills and resources to deliver the best, sustainable results.

- **Stewardship:** We are passionate about leaving things better than we found them.[4]

Jenkins deeply believes in this values-based approach to building organizations, as he persistently connects leadership, culture, and performance. But despite his admirable energy and resilience, the pursuit of these honorable objectives is beset with problems. Changing organizational culture has a timescale that ill fits the discipline of quarterly reporting. Large investors want change and improved performance quickly, but embedding values-based authentic leadership takes time. In addition, even among his most senior colleagues, there are reservoirs of cynicism that hold back the desire for change. In short, rediscovering authentic organizations is very tough.

Another example is the recent revival of the consulting firm A. T. Kearney.[5] Established in Chicago in the late 1920s, the firm developed a distinctive culture over the next thirty years under the leadership of Tom Kearney. It took particular pride in the way it engaged with clients and offered not just advice but also on-the-ground assistance with change implementation.

"We didn't just talk to chairmen and CEOs—we partnered with the businesses . . . our clients valued us because they saw us as real people, truly collaborating with them to fully implement high-impact programs," says partner Phil Morgan. Adds partner Gary Singer: "We tried to be simple and direct. Our focus is on working *with*, not working on, clients."

The firm globalized and grew substantially in the 1980s and 1990s and was acquired by IT giant EDS in 1995. Initially this combination was tremendously successful, but as the EDS core business deteriorated, so did the combination's impact on A. T. Kearney—there was a significant loss of talent and the leaders craved the spirit and advantages of a partnership. In response, 177 partners from twenty-six countries bought out the firm in 2005 and set about "reclaiming" it. This was a significant personal risk for each them, "but they saw the opportunity to create something special that could not be replicated elsewhere," says Morgan.

Since the buyback, revenues and the number of partners have increased by 55 and 59 percent, respectively. No partner owns more than 1 percent of the equity; each partner has one vote only; and any partner can nominate any other for membership of the global board. Within this exceptionally democratic culture, individuals are encouraged to be entrepreneurial, drive results, and help build the most admired global firm.

If the authentic organization is one where you can express your authentic self, then A. T. Kearney has created a structure and culture to support just that. With its "Vision 2020" initiative launched in 2013, the firm looks to the future by building on the past with an aim to become the industry's "most admired" firm—by "building on our rich heritage and the accomplishments of those who preceded us," according to Vision 2020 guidelines. "Their story—our story—is proof positive that it's within our DNA to exceed all expectations."[6]

So here is a firm guiding its future by careful and deliberate reference to its authentic origins. It has recently produced a well-researched history, "The A. T. Kearney Story," and sent it to all employees "so they can share it with their families—we want them to feel part of the story too," says Phil Morgan.

Is the story complete? Of course not. The firm remains smaller than several of its competitors and must continue to work hard to distinguish itself from the likes of McKinsey, Bain, and BCG, as well as the big four audit firms. It aspires to be the most admired among this competitive set, to double in size by the year 2020, and to be among the top three wherever it competes. But the determination to tell it how it is (what the firm calls "essential rightness"), to democratically connect partners (and their families), and to stay true to founding values indicates an organization that, in our view, is making real progress in terms of recapturing a shared sense of authenticity, community, meaning, and honesty.

In the next section we offer some pragmatic advice on how the ideal organization may be realized—be it created, sustained, or recaptured.

Building a Better Workplace

Crafting authentic organizations is a tough task. While conducting this research we studied some great organizations that are struggling purposefully to build great places to work. None of them have found it easy. And in this last substantive chapter we don't want to in any way imply that there is some kind of simple mechanical plan that will always work. Organizations just aren't like that. We do think, however, that we can identify some critical success factors that make efforts to build great organizations more likely to succeed, such as the support of *top management* and the presence of strong organizational *performance drivers*. We will look at each of these in turn, as well as at a number of caveats to keep in mind on your way to fundamental change.

Support from the Top

The first critical success factor is the resilient support of top management, who need to be both cognitively convinced of the benefits of building great organizations and emotionally committed to the long-term nature of organizational development. At Novo Nordisk and at Arup, the support from the top is constant and palpable. It is both intellectual and affective.

Conversely, top managers cannot abdicate responsibility. Take the pursuit of difference, for example ("D" in our DREAMS organization). If this pursuit becomes a project located in the HR department, it's almost doomed to failure. It becomes perceived as yet another diversity initiative and often runs into a wall of silent cynicism. That is why the expression of difference needs to be embraced widely and supported from the top of the organization. Arguments for it must be clearly based on the business imperatives of building creativity and innovation. Similarly, if radical honesty ("R" in DREAMS) becomes an issue for the communications function, it's unlikely to be viewed as anything more than another form of spin. If extra value ("E") is conceived of as the remit of the training department, it is similarly doomed. Some organizations see building authenticity ("A") like a kind of branding exercise, with the marketing department to the fore. They make the mistake of thinking that authenticity can be established with clever tag lines. This is simply never the case. And if meaning ("M") becomes forever related to driving up engagement scores, organizations never tackle the real issues. Finally, don't leave building simple rules ("S") to the legal and compliance departments. They are trained to develop complexity!

Driven to Perform

Clearly another critical success factor is that the elements of DREAMS are based on strong organizational performance drivers. And this is as true for public sector and not-for-profit organizations as it is for the classic capitalist enterprise. We have also discovered that it is almost impossible to work on all of this at once. So where should you start? As we hope we made clear in chapter 1, definitely do not begin with "diversity initiatives" that only increase the representation of particular groups while having zero effect on the company's true diversity of thought and mind-set. Rather, a critical reason to work on *difference* is the imperative to increase creativity and innovation. It's why the difference agenda at Novo Nordisk is so critical. The organization seeks to do nothing less than change the world of diabetes. For Arup, creativity is one of the very reasons it exists, and this helps to explain why it has so successfully built difference into its culture.

You should pursue *radical honesty* when you are confronted with a culture characterized by gossip, rumor, and negative networks. Sadly, these are often found in large organizations. The BBC discovered that the most frequently cited source of information about the organization was gossip and rumor, followed by the trade unions. The organization responded with a fundamental reexamination of the way it communicated with its employees. It made a promise to tell people what was going on before they heard it from anyone else. It rejuvenated the channels of communication, relying much less on the old world of the staff newspaper and more on immediate internet-based communication. Recent scandals, however, point to another reason to pursue radical honesty—when the external view of your organization has become negative, damaging your reputational capital. Many financial services firms have faced just such a challenge since the crash of 2008, as have pharmaceutical companies like Eli Lilly and Merck in response to the Oraflex and Vioxx scandals.

Address *extra value* when you are experiencing two possible symptoms. The first is when the company has trouble retaining its best people. As Chris Satterthwaite, chief executive of marketing services company Chime, remarks: "Your best people leave when they know the value they add is greater than the value the organization adds to them." In the tight labor markets of the emerging economies, this is often a vital issue. For Novo Nordisk in India or LVMH in China, for example, the ability to add value through personal development is a far more powerful device for attracting and keeping talent than simple financial incentives.

The second sign that an injection of extra value is needed is low mobility within the organization. In other words, the people who do stay become stuck in their jobs. A case in point is a pharmaceutical company with which we worked—one of the best pharma companies in the world, actually, in terms of both market capitalization and track record of innovation. Although its "pilot plant" operation was performing satisfactorily, in the culture of this organization "satisfactorily" was clearly not good enough. Interviewing staff members, we learned that many had been doing the same job for more than ten years. That is when we suggested much higher levels of internal mobility—put simply, people were given different jobs to perform. Over the course of eighteen months, performance improved dramatically. It taught us a stark lesson; it's not always a good thing to leave people in the same role, even when their performance is satisfactory. Small changes can have big effects.

Authenticity may be a start point where it has become unclear what the organization stands for. Ironically, this is sometimes signaled by a succession of hastily rewritten mission statements. Earlier we referred to the Dilbert Mission Statement Generator, a spoof device for the production of mission statements. In some organizations, people feel as if they have been subjected to just such a process. Authenticity, however, is achieved not through fancy catchphrases but rather a connection with the past, clarity and continuity of purpose, and exemplary leadership. Organizations like BMW, Novo Nordisk, New York Life, and Heineken pass these tests with flying colors.

Turn to *meaning* when you are confronted with low engagement scores and silo mentalities. These symptoms may tell you something about the way jobs are designed and organizations are structured. Sadly, the legacy of Taylorism still hangs over both jobs and organizational design, even in companies that have sprung up in recent years to exploit the internet for commercial advantage. But low engagement can also result from a loss of a sense of community. As careers become characterized by higher rates of mobility and often mixed bursts of employment and self-employment, corporate communities have fragmented. New technologies have also contributed to the problem by encouraging the growth of virtual teams and reducing opportunities for face-to-face contact. As Henry Mintzberg points out, "Tellingly, some of the companies we admire most—Toyota, Semco (Brazil), Mondragon (a Basque federation of cooperatives), Pixar, and so on—typically have this strong sense of community."[7]

Finally, you might begin with *simple rules* when the organization seems to be shrouded in a web of complexity, where people experience their work as overly constrained and the prevailing culture is "it's more than my job is worth"—that is, people merely fulfill the minimum requirements of their role and are afraid to exercise discretion. Attempting to address this issue is not a new phenomenon—think of Jack Welch's famous crusade at GE or the resurrection of Southwest Airlines. More recently, Unilever has dramatically streamlined its brand portfolio, enabling the organization to focus on superbrands. But lessons can also perhaps be learned from some surprising places. Mumbai's legendary *dabbawallas*, for example, who deliver home-cooked food to thousands of office workers, by bicycle and by train, are able to sustain their astounding service record (delivering 130,000 lunch boxes per day throughout one of the world's most populous cities) through adherence to simple codes. These contain just enough information for people to know where to deliver. Delta Airlines recently redesigned its boarding passes in a way that mirrors the *dabbawallas'* approach.[8]

Caveat *Emptor*

On the road to pursuing the organization of your dreams, certainly you will require resilience, courage, and cleverness. But remaining mindful of the following points will minimize disillusionment and frustration.

Pursuing one DREAMS element may undermine another. Novo Nordisk is justly proud of its Danish roots. Despite its stellar growth in the last ten years, it remains a fundamentally Danish company, headquartered in Copenhagen with the overwhelming majority of its senior management composed of Danish nationals. Not surprisingly, such adherence to its roots (authenticity) makes the pursuit of difference difficult. While the company has no trouble grasping cognitively and appreciating the value of pursuing difference, the company DNA makes it hard to implement. It's not just that they are Danish, and male, it's that a certain style of thinking—fact based, implementation biased—dominates.

In contrast, a company where excessive difference reigns can create its own problems in terms of adherence to shared purpose, and may undermine attempts to stick to simple rules. For example, at their worst, complex matrix systems may house highly specialized technical experts whose local obsessions may limit shared values and organizational cohesion. This is the price that many knowledge-based firms simply have to pay to achieve innovation. This is true for the giants of modern technology such as Microsoft and Cisco. But it is also true for creative cultural enterprises like museums, opera houses, and haute couture maisons.

Finally, it is possible that an organization that practices radical honesty may express that candor in ways that are shocking for some, producing disengagement and loss of meaning. For example, as the major banks have attempted to repair their reputational capital by openly admitting their mistakes over subprime mortgages and the LIBOR scandal, staff lower down the hierarchy who have been struggling with day-to-day operations may feel that all of their efforts have lost meaning. They feel it's become a company they don't recognize—"not the one we joined."

Don't make promises you can't keep. For organizations trying to create and sustain authenticity, it's important to acknowledge the costs that sometimes come with trying to do the right thing— and the difficulties that organizations will surely face when trying to keep their promises. The story of a whistle-blower at EY in 2014 illustrates the personal cost of highlighting an issue, as well as how EY as an organization is challenged to stay aligned with its regulatory obligations and professed purpose. The incident concerned conflict gold (allegedly procured under questionable circumstances) and the supply chain practices of Kaloti, the Middle East's largest gold refiner. The whistle-blower—a Dubai-based EY partner—resigned over the incident. Although EY denies wrongdoing, when the story was featured in a TV news program, the organization's promise was challenged.[9]

EY's desire to "build a better working world" is without doubt sincere and fully supported; indeed—from our direct experience in the UK—it is strongly driven by its managing partner. But controlling a large multinational professional services firm will always leave you open to possible challenge.

These obstacles are by no means unique to EY. They arise whenever organizations make claims about quality, ethics, and efficacy that they are seen to be challenged to deliver. Think about automobile manufacturers, banks, and pharma companies. In each of these sectors, delivery on promises turns out to be harder than it seemed.

Don't try to do too much. We know that most culture change programs fail. Why is this? Frequently it is because objectives are excessively ambitious. The harsh reality is that cultures cannot be "managed." Some aspects will always be virtually unmanageable. Go to work for your company's subsidiary in Tokyo and you will be unlikely to change the course of the last two thousand years of Japanese history during your three-year stint. Become the dean of a leading business school and you will have to accept many of the norms and practices of academic professors. Certain aspects of culture are more or less givens.

But clearly, cultures can and do change. They will evolve—whether you like it or not. And leaders can influence that evolution largely through their own behaviors. You can see this process at work in owner-founder start-ups. The actions of entrepreneurs can fundamentally shape the emerging culture—as they are, for example, at Supercell. The vigilance of executives of steadfast, long-standing companies like Johnson & Johnson can ensure that the Credo values evolve and develop in ways that support the continuing success of the business.

Cultural "transformations" can also be achieved—but rarely if too much is attempted too soon. All the evidence indicates that success comes from focusing initiatives (as we already have discussed) and, crucially, from building on fundamental defining features that are at the root of organizations and which often explain their early successes. As we have said, this doesn't require age—Apple, Google, Microsoft, and Cisco, giants of the modern global economy, are all relatively modern, yet they have strong roots.

As we recounted in an earlier chapter, Paul Polman, Unilever's CEO, is credited with transforming the culture since his arrival in 2009. He describes his objectives as "audacious." Indeed they are—to double the size of the company while halving its carbon footprint. Yet he traces the company's contemporary ambitions back to its roots. Begun in the nineteenth century, Unilever has a long history of "doing the right thing," Polman says. For example, when William Lever (later Lord Lever-Hulme) started the company, Britain was mired in deaths associated with poor hygiene. "So he invented bar soap," he says, "not to make more money, but because in Victorian England one out of two babies didn't make it past year one. That established the company's values, and we need to build on them." Therefore, before Polman launched Unilever's most recent plan to build sustainability into its supply chain, he connected the new efforts with the historic values of the organization. When the project was launched, "only 10% of our materials were sourced sustainably. Now, after just one year with new stretch targets, we're sourcing 24% sustainable."[10] Audacious—yes; connected with the past—certainly.

For its part, the game company Supercell has thus far managed to keep from overstretching itself as an organization, even as it has added offices in San Francisco, Seoul, and Tokyo. "The more successful you are, the more difficult it is," cofounder and CEO Ilkka Paananen told us. "Communication becomes harder. Sustaining the culture is a challenge." And inevitably there comes a time when hard choices must be made. "If someone doesn't fit, then you have to say goodbye. If a project doesn't live up to our standards of craftsmanship, then it has to be killed." He also says the company has resisted enormous pressure from the board and externally to grow—too fast, in Paananen's assessment. "We have offers all the time to use the brand in movies, amusement parks, etc. And we have to say no."

Can You Regulate a Dream?

Since the financial crash of 2008—which rapidly became the biggest economic crisis since 1929—there have been frequent and vociferous calls for ever more invasive regulation of our organizational lives. Apologists for the banking system argue that such regulation inhibits innovation and ultimately reduces global liquidity. Old-style corporatists argue equally forcibly that firms cannot be trusted to regulate themselves and push for more powerful government mechanisms of control.

Our view is that "good" regulation has clear purpose and is appropriate to social context. There is a more fundamental point to make about this: markets are never free of their social context. For them to work effectively, they are supported by what Durkheim calls "the non-contractual elements of contract"—a set of tacit assumptions that underpin social and economic relationships.

It is also true that even though we speak of a global capitalist system, capitalism takes many forms. Consider the difference between the Anglo-American version and the currently rather successful Nordic version or the rather state-sponsored capitalism characteristic of Singapore. It is naive in the extreme not to consider the social context in which economies are based. It is perhaps unsurprising therefore that many of our persistent examples in this book—Novo Nordisk, Arup, Supercell—are located in "high trust" Scandinavian societies, leading us to believe that perhaps bureaucracy functions best in such societies.

Legislating for other aspects of the DREAMS organization is also problematic. As we discussed earlier in chapter 1, rule books on diversity are not a guarantee of the fundamental types of difference required to produce, for example, creativity and innovation. Similarly, disclosure rules will not guarantee honesty, nor will equal-opportunities legislation necessarily produce fairness. The best they can do is provide a backdrop against which human agents cooperatively produce great organizations.

While we were researching this book, we attended a conference of US hedge fund managers. This was about one year after the crisis of 2008. The conference was full of very clever people working out ways in which they could beat the regulators. We were immediately struck that no matter how complex and invasive regulation was, they would find a way around it.

A curious observation is that imposed regulation simply generates deviance. Human beings have remarkable capacity to break or bend the rules. Sociological studies of schools, factories, hospitals, prisons, and universities bear witness to the ability of individuals and groups to find ways around rule systems that they perceive as unfair and imposed. Such regulation won't work. Good regulations fit the context and rest on trust.

Next, in the conclusion, we look at how each of the DREAMS aspects offers distinctive elements that foster high-performing organizations—critical if we are to weather challenging economic times. Sometimes employees are viewed as passive recipients of organizational life. We challenge you to build organizations in which individuals feel they can make choices that enable them to do their best work and be proud of of it.

Toward More Authentic Organizations

We began our work for this book by asking people to describe their dream organization—one that feels authentic and within which it is possible for one's best self to emerge. In these chapters we have synthesized these ideal organizational qualities and have shown how some workplaces are making the elements of the dream real, inspiring the rest of us in the process.

Each of the DREAMS elements brings distinctive benefits.

Organizations that give scope for people to be themselves accept—and often celebrate—personal *difference*. This is not an easy thing to achieve. Organizations are full of both formal mechanisms and more subtle, informal processes that produce similarity and conformity. Handling diversity is not easy. It requires tolerance, open-mindedness, and a willingness to address possible conflict. But there is a major pay-off. *Allowing people to be them-selves generates commitment—and fosters creativity.* Remember how the shop floor workers at Waitrose feel about their work? And how Arup looks for people who "don't fit" as a way of fueling the company's ability to create the unimaginable?

Radical honesty is less of a choice these days. A social media world and a workforce tired of spin both point to the need to open up. Organizational needs to share information fast—and regulatory demands for transparency—add to the pressure. So organizations are pushed to share information, both inside and outside. But again there is a distinctive benefit from the proactive and speedy candor that characterizes radical honesty. *It facilitates an understanding and awareness of what is going on.* It helps explain why things are as they are, or why they must change. Neither status quo nor new modus operandi are likely to be accepted by those trapped by a communication blackout. Remember Novo Nordisk: not all the news is comfortable, but proactive processes for sharing enable individuals to make sense of circumstances, good and bad.

The benefit of magnifying strengths is that people are developed. If you build human capital, you add *extra value* to people rather than extract it. This equation is unquestioned, it seems, in the treatment of elites—in professional occupations and cutting-edge, knowledge-based organizations. But value can be added in many ways and for many people. McDonald's may be critiqued for its work processes or wage levels, but its investment in training of frontline workers is exemplary; the LOCOG volunteers were lifted by the opportunity—and in turn they elevated the entire Olympic and Paralympic experience in London.

Organizations that foster *authenticity* know what they stand for. They are distinctive in terms of their identity and roots, their values, and their leadership. They provide people with a reason to believe. They are unlikely to be places that succumb to quick fixes or that produce and reproduce one mission statement after another. They have a purpose that is more than "shareholder value." *Those who work for authentic organizations—like New York Life—are proud of what they do.* But perhaps the major positive is trust—a long time in the making, but easily destroyed.

Where work feels meaningful, individuals experience a sense of purpose. They can find intrinsic *meaning* in their jobs, in the way their work connects to others and the broader work community in which they are employed. Ultimately, they can connect what they do to an overarching cause. The BMW engineer knows why (s)he is going to work. Do you?

Finally—and perhaps paradoxically—*organizations that establish simple rules create the conditions for freedom.* As we point out, this does not equate to anarchy. Rules are inevitable—but the point is to make them fair, clear, and workable. In doing so it is possible to maximize discretion and freedom to act, in ways that are beneficial for all. Remember the idealism of the House of St Barnabas or the Netflix belief that individuals will "do the right thing"?

Put together these multiple benefits—commitment, creativity, understanding, personal development, trust, purpose, and freedom—and you have created the fundamentals that underpin engagement at work. And we know that engagement is correlated with performance.

The dream organization, then, is also the high-performing organization.

But don't for a moment imagine that engagement is the panacea for our organizational ills. It may yet come to be seen as another superficial attempt to increase the discretionary effort of employees. If engagement is to lead to really significant change, it must be allied to a more fundamental rethink of our organizational lives. It is a central contention of this book that organizations, in all their forms, constitute a major determinant of healthy lives and healthy societies. Sociologist Amitai Etzioni captures their centrality as follows:

> We are born in organizations, educated by organizations, and most of us spend much of our lives working in organizations. We spend much of our leisure time paying, playing and praying in organizations. Most of us will die in organizations and, when the time comes for burial, the largest organization of them all—the State—must grant official permission.[1]

It follows from Etzioni's insight that if our organizational lives turn sour, then so too will our personal lives. Rethinking our organizations is not just about profit, efficiency, or effectiveness; it's about crafting recipes for good societies. What the respondents in our research have asked for is organizations where they can be themselves, know the truth, grow, believe in the purpose, and be given the freedom to pursue it. We have reported examples of organizations that are making tremendous strides in these directions, but by both temperament and training we are prone to pessimism. We see the twin challenges of reinventing capitalism and resisting bureaucracy as enormous tasks. And of course, many people are constrained by the organizations they experience— they seem to have no choice. Perhaps, as in so many aspects of our social lives, aspects of choice, chance, and constraint are all at play. We simply observe that, increasingly, people wish to exercise choice.

Even so, as we were finishing our writing, we took one last look at our interview notes. This is what some people said about their work and their organizations:

> I am proud of our supermarket—and I do all I can to make sure that people can buy the food they want. And sometimes they try something new! (Waitrose, department head, UK)

We run the systems for some of the biggest companies in the world. When they are in danger of crashing, our engineers do everything to keep things running. It's exciting and it works. (Cisco, engineering VP, California)

Me and my colleagues work really hard to make the best cars in the world. I love watching a 6 series roll off the line. I know someone is going to have the drive of their life! (BMW, production line worker, Germany)

We do everything to ensure that we practice the highest professional standards. I seek to exemplify professional integrity in everything I do. (PwC, audit partner, London)

As a long-time Unilever person, I'm drawn back to a line from our statement of corporate purpose—"Unilever exists to meet the everyday needs of everyday people everywhere." It gives me a real sense of a shared human experience. (Unilever, senior marketer, India)

Our hospital stands for all that is best in patient care. Our staff are caring and expert. It is simply a joy to work for an organization with such a noble purpose. (Hospital administrator, Boston)

The way we see it, all of these people are answering the same difficult question. Now it's your turn. Take a close look at your organization, and ask the all-important question: Why should anyone work here?

Methods and Diagnostic Instrument

I n our research for this book we have conducted interviews, run company workshops, and gathered observational data from our hands-on consulting work. All the organizations where we have worked and gathered data are listed in our acknowledgments.

Many social sciences have developed a tendency to rely on quantitative data and modeling techniques, often derived from economics. We are sociologists brought up in a rather different tradition. We were taught that the key skills are observation and listening. As a consequence, we are both compulsive note takers! Many of the examples in the book, therefore, are drawn from direct observation, formal and informal interviewing, and the many notes we make when working with organizations. These methods are linked to a theoretical stance that stresses the role that individuals and groups play in the creation and re-creation of the social world.

We have also, however, developed a diagnostic instrument. Initially this constituted a simple checklist of questions. This format was used in our earlier article in the *Harvard Business Review*, "Creating the Best Workplace on Earth" (May 2013). For this book we have edited some of the questions and used a scale to help you build a slightly richer picture of your organization.

Consider these questions:

Where are you strongest?

Where do you need to improve?

Where is the best place to start?

Where will you need to make trade-offs?

---

1 = Strongly Disagree

2 = Disagree

3 = Neither Agree Nor Disagree

4 = Agree

5 = Strongly Agree

Difference

I can be myself here

_____ I am the same person at home as I am at work.

_____ I am comfortable being myself.

_____ We are all encouraged to express our differences.

_____ People who think differently from most do well here.

_____ Passion is encouraged, even when it leads to conflict.

_____ More than one type of person fits in here.

Radical Honesty

You're told what is really going on

_____   We are all told the real story.

_____   Information is not manipulated.

_____   It is not disloyal to say something negative.

_____   My manager wants to hear bad news.

_____   Many channels of communication are available to us.

_____   I feel comfortable signing my name to comments I make.

Extra Value

Your strengths are magnified

_____   I am given the chance to develop.

_____   Every employee is given the chance to develop.

_____   The best people want to perform here.

_____   The weakest performers can see a path to improvement.

_____   Compensation is fairly distributed throughout the organization.

_____   We generate value for ourselves by adding value to others.

Authenticity

You are proud of where we're coming from and what we stand for

_____ I know what we stand for.

_____ I value what we stand for.

_____ I want to exceed my current duties.

_____ Profit is not our overriding goal.

_____ I am accomplishing something worthwhile.

_____ I like to tell people where I work.

Meaning

The work makes sense

_____ My job is meaningful to me.

_____ My duties make sense to me.

_____ My work gives me energy and pleasure.

_____ I understand how my job fits with everyone else's.

_____ Everyone's job is necessary.

_____ At work we share a common cause.

Simple Rules

We believe in the rules

_____ We keep things simple.

_____ The rules are clear and apply equally to everyone.

_____ I know what the rules are for.

_____ Everyone knows what the rules are for.

_____ We, as an organization, resist unnecessary rules and paperwork.

_____ Authority is respected.

Any item scoring 1 or 2 is worth attention. Any dimension with an overall score below 18 suggests this area requires improvement.

Notes

Introduction

1. According to a May 2012 report by Catalyst, a US-based research organization, the US labor force currently spans four generations. Catalyst, *Catalyst Quick Take: Generations in the Workplace in the United States and Canada* (New York: Catalyst, 2012), http://www.catalyst.org/knowledge/generations-workplace-united-states-canada.

2. The survey spanned forty thousand employers in forty-two countries and territories. ManpowerGroup, "2013 Talent Shortage Survey: United States," http://www.manpowergroup.us/campaigns/talent-shortage-2013/pdf/TSS_MPG_NA_2013_vertical_061713-zz.pdf.

3. Rob Goffee and Gareth Jones, *Why Should Anyone Be Led by You?* (Boston: Harvard Business School Press, 2006).

4. Patrick Hosking, "The 'Yes' Men at HSBC Mislay Their Moral Compass," *The Times* (London), November 26, 2014.

5. Ibid.

6. Circle Research, "Exploring the Shift in Employee Expectations," The Perspective Series, Circle Research with Vodafone UK, 2012; Stephen Sweet and Peter Meiskins, *Changing Contours of Work* (Los Angeles: Sage, 2013).

7. Francis Fukuyama, *The End of History and the Last Man* (New York: Free Press, 1992).

8. Erik Brynjolfsson and Andrew McAfee, *The Second Machine Age: Work, Progress, and Prosperity in a Time of Brilliant Technologies* (New York: W.W. Norton, 2014).

9. Eric Schmidt and Jonathan Rosenberg, *How Google Works* (New York: Grand Central Publishing, 2014).

10. Richard Scase and Robert Goffee, *Reluctant Managers* (London: Routledge, 1989).

11. Rob Goffee and Gareth Jones, *Clever: Leading Your Smartest, Most Creative People* (Boston: Harvard Business Review Press, 2009), 168.

12. This was a point we made a few years back in our book *The Character*

of a Corporation (New York: Collins, 1998)—which was a sustained attempt to describe different cultures for different contexts.

13. Hay Group, "Employee Engagement Global Survey," 2012.

14. AON Hewitt, "2012 Trends in Global Employee Engagement," 2012.

Chapter 1

1. Emile Durkheim, *The Division of Labour in Society* (New York: Free Press, 1984).

2. Anthony Giddens, *Emile Durkheim: Selected Writings* (Cambridge, UK: Cambridge University Press, 1972), 8.

3. George Homans, *The Human Group* (London: Routledge and Kegan Paul, 1951).

4. Rob Goffee and Richard Scase, "Proprietorial Control in Family Firms: Some Function of Quasi-Organic Management Systems," *Journal of Management Studies* 22, no. 1 (1985).

5. Thomas J. Peters and Robert H. Waterman Jr., *In Search of Excellence* (New York: Harper & Row, 1982).

6. Walker Review of Corporate Governance on the UK Banking Industry, 2009.

7. Alan Fox, *Beyond Contract: Work, Power and Trust Relationships* (London: Faber and Faber, 1974).

8. Rob Goffee and Gareth Jones, "Why Boards Go Wrong," *Management Today*, September 2011.

9. Homans, *The Human Group*, 115.

10. Research by Dan Cable, London Business School; Daniel M. Cable and Virginia S. Kay, "Striving for Self-Verification during Organizational Entry," *Academy of Management Journal* 55, no. 2 (April 2012): 360–380.

11. We first used these diagnostic questions informally as part of our interviewing process. This developed into a simple questionnaire using a tick box format—individuals were asked to simply check off the statements that applied. This was the format used in our previously published article, "Creating the Best Workplace on Earth" (*Harvard Business Review,* May 2013). For this book we have used similar questions but converted them to a scale. In our commentary on responses in this chapter and throughout the book, we are broadly generalizing from all three types of response. As we report, some elements of the DREAMS organization regularly attract more positive responses. However, in general, "strong" or "positive" scores tend to equate to around 60 percent satisfaction levels; less "strong" or "positive" are around 35 to 40 percent. Hence our suggestion that a score below 18 (averaging

3 or below on six 5-point scale questions) suggests considerable scope for improvement.

12. Philip Dilley was group chairman of Arup 2009–2014; he now serves as an Arup trustee.

Chapter 2

1. Details on the BP oil spill drawn in part from the following sources: S. Elizabeth Birnbaum and Jacqueline Savitz, "The Deepwater Horizon Threat," *New York Times*, April 17, 2014; http://en.wikipedia.org/wiki/Reactions_to_ the_Deepwater_Horizon_oil_spill.

2. Reported in http://en.wikipedia.org/wiki/Reactions_to_the_ Deepwater_Horizon_oil_spill, referencing Tim Webb, "BP Boss Admits Job on the Line over Gulf Oil Spill," *The Guardian* (London), May 13, 2010.

3. Kirsten Korosec, "BP and the Oil Spill: What Tony Hayward Is Telling His Employees," *CBSNews,com*, CBS Moneywatch, May 20, 2010, http://www .cbsnews.com/news/bp-and-the-oil-spill-what-ceo-tony-hayward-is-telling-his-employees/.

4. Ibid.

5. Eric Schmidt and Jonathan Rosenberg, *How Google Works* (New York: Grand Central Publishing, 2014), 175–176.

6. Edelman Trust Barometer Annual Global Study, 2014, shows trust levels at an all-time historic low.

7. Sean Poulter, "Tesco Rapped over Misleading Horsemeat Ad: Supermarket Accused of Trying to Fool Customers by Spreading Blame for Scandal," *DailyMail.com*, September 3, 2013, http://www.dailymail.co.uk/ news/article-2410618/Tescos-misleading-horsemeat-ad-Supermarket-accused-trying-pass-blame.html.

8. Jürgen Habermas, *The Theory of Communicative Action*, Vol. 1, trans. Thomas McCarthy (Boston: Beacon Press, 1984).

9. David Runciman, *Political Hypocrisy* (Princeton, NJ: Princeton University Press, 2008); Niccolò Machiavelli, *The Prince* (London: Penguin, 1961).

10. Interestingly, attempts to tighten corporate taxation rules in the UK have become known as "the Google tax."

11. See, among other sources, "MPs Attack Amazon, Google and Starbucks Over Tax Avoidance," *The Guardian*, December 3, 2012.

12. "Starbucks to Pay £20 Million in Tax over Next Two Years after Customer Revolt," *The Guardian*, December 6, 2012.

13. Details from Wikipedia and other websites, including Ben Brumfield and Holly Yan, "MH370 Report: Mixed Messages Ate Up Time Before Official

Search Initiated," *CNN.com*, May 2, 2014, http://www.cnn.com/2014/05/01/world/asia/malaysia-airlines-plane-report/.

14. "MH370 Report: Mixed Messages Ate Up Time before Official Search Initiated," CNN.com, http://www.cnn.com/2014/05/01/world/asia/malaysia-airlines-plane-report/ (accessed May 9, 2014).

15. "MH370 Continues to Be a Priority for Malaysian Government," statement by YB Dato' Sri Liow Tiong Lai, Minister of Transport, Malaysia, August 9, 2014, http://www.malaysiaairlines.com/mh370.

16. Rob Goffee and Gareth Jones, *Clever: Leading Your Smartest, Most Creative People* (Boston: Harvard Business Review Press, 2009); Jay R. Galbraith, *Designing Complex Organizations* (Reading, MA: Addison-Wesley, 1973).

17. Maria Halkias, "Rock-Solid Turnaround," *New York Times*, September 8, 2013, D1.

Chapter 3

1. John Purcell, *Understanding the People and Performance Link* (London: CIPD Publishing, 2003).

2. Alan Fox, *Beyond Contract: Work, Power and Trust Relationships* (London: Faber and Faber, 1974).

3. R. Strack, J. M. Caye, C. Linden, H. Quiros, and P. Haen, "From Capability to Profitability: Realizing the Value of People Management," *BCG Perspectives*, August 2012.

4. Frederick Winslow Taylor, *The Principles of Scientific Management* (New York: Harper & Bros., 1911).

5. Donald Roy, "Quota Restriction and Goldbricking in a Machine Shop," *American Journal of Sociology* 57, no. 5 (1952).

6. Adolf Berle and Gardiner Means, *The Modern Corporation and Private Property* (Piscataway, NJ: Transaction Publishers, 1932).

7. "How Long Does the Average Share Last? Just 22 Seconds," *The Telegraph*, January 18, 2012, http://www.telegraph.co.uk/finance/personalfinance/investing/9021946/How-long-does-the-average-share-holding-last-Just-22-seconds.html.

8. Michael Lewis, *Flash Boys: A Wall Street Revolt* (New York: W. W. Norton, 2014).

9. Dominic Rushe, "Over 100 Arrested Near McDonald's Headquarters in Protest over Low Pay," *The Guardian*, May 21, 2014; "Notice of 2014 Annual Shareholders' Meeting and Proxy Statement," McDonald's Corporation, http://www.aboutmcdonalds.com/content/dam/AboutMcDonalds/Investors/2014%20Proxy_Web%20Version.PDF (Proxy, p. 26). McDonald's

position is that any minimum wage increase should be implemented over time so that the impact on owners of small and medium-sized businesses—the majority—is manageable.

10. J. W. Hunt, *Managing People at Work*, 2nd ed. (London: McGraw-Hill, 1986).

11. G. Becker, *Human Capital*, 3rd ed. (Chicago: University of Chicago Press, 1993).

12. This concept finds its most clear exposition in Pierre Bourdieu's *Distinction: A Social Critique of the Judgment of Taste* (Cambridge, MA: Harvard University Press, 1984).

13. Zoë Corbyn, "Is San Francisco Losing Its Soul?" *The Guardian*, February 23, 2014, http://www.theguardian.com/world/2014/feb/23/is-san-francisco-losing-its-soul.

14. Caille Millner, "Why We're Invisible to Google Bus Riders," *San Francisco Chronicle*, April 26, 2013.

15. Adam Bryant, "Corner Office: Sometimes, You Can Have the Cake and Eat It, Too," *New York Times*, September 8, 2013, Sunday Business, 2.

16. Zhang Rumin, "Raising Haier," *Harvard Business Review,* February 2007.

Chapter 4

1. As cited by Nancy Lublin in "How to Write a Mission Statement That Isn't Dumb," *Fast Company,* November 2009, http://www.fastcompany .com/1400930/how-write-mission-statement-isnt-dumb.

2. Thomas J. Peters and Robert H. Waterman Jr., *In Search of Excellence* (New York: Harper & Row, 1982).

3. Cited in New York Life internal documents.

4. Cited in *BBC News Magazine* online, February 18, 2013.

5. "Manchester United agree new £750million sponsorship deal with Adidas," *Telegraph Sport* online, July 14, 2014, http://www.telegraph.co.uk/sport/football/teams/manchester-united/10966026/Manchester-United-agree-new-750million-sponsorship-deal-with-Adidas.html.

6. Rob Goffee and Gareth Jones, *The Character of a Corporation*, 2nd ed. (London: Profile Books, 2003), 73.

7. Peter Foster, "Gree Electric's Dong Mingzhu: Why China's Leading Businesswoman Doesn't Do Holidays," *The Telegraph*, August 24, 2009; Didi Kirsten Tatlow, "Setting the Pace with Toughness," *New York Times*, January 26, 2011.

8. C. Wright Mills, *The Sociological Imagination* (Oxford, UK: Oxford University Press, 1959).

Chapter 5

1. July 9, 1970, "Key Speech," http://www.arup.com/Home/Publications/ The_Key_Speech.aspx, now widely held by insiders as the Arup corporate bible.

2. Studs Terkel, *Working* (New York: Pantheon, 1974).

3. This research ranges from the early motivations theorists such as Maslow and Hertzberg all the way through to contemporary interest in engagement and creativity. For a review of the classic sociological traditions, see Mike Rose, *Industrial Behaviour*, 2nd ed. (Harmondsworth, UK: Penguin, 1988). For more recent interest in creativity, see Teresa M. Amibele and Steven J. Kramer, *The Progress Principle* (Boston: Harvard Business Review Press, 2011); and for engagement see Christopher Rice, Fraser Marlow, and Mary Ann Masarech, *The Engagement Equation* (Hoboken, NJ: Wiley, 2012).

4. Alain de Botton, Investec lecture, Investec website (undated); but also see his book *The Pleasures and Sorrows of Work* (New York: Vintage Books, 2010).

5. Theo Nichols, *Living with Capitalism* (London: Routledge and Kegan Paul, 1977), 16.

6. Donald Roy, "Quota Restriction and Goldbricking in a Machine Shop," *American Journal of Sociology* 57 (1952): 427–442; Donald Roy, "Efficiency and 'The Fix': Informal Intergroup Relations in a Piecework Machine Shop," *American Journal of Sociology* 60, no. 3 (1954).

7. Donald Roy, "'Banana Time': Job Satisfaction and Informal Interaction," *Human Organization,* 18, no. 4 (1959): 158–168.

8. Miklos Haraszti, *Worker in a Worker's State* (London: Penguin, 1977).

9. Dov Seidman, *How: Why How We Do Anything Means Everything* (Hoboken, NJ: Wiley, 2007).

10. Charles Handy, *The Age of Unreason* (Boston: Harvard Business School Press, 1990).

11. Richard Sennett, *The Corrosion of Character* (New York: W. W. Norton, 1998), 148.

12. Rob Goffee and Gareth Jones, *The Character of a Corporation* (New York: HarperCollins, 1998).

13. Ibid.

14. Thomas J. Peters and Robert H. Waterman Jr., *In Search of Excellence* (New York: Harper & Row, 1982).

15. John Kay, *Obliquity* (New York: Penguin, 2010).

16. Alexander Solzhenitsyn, *One Day in the Life of Ivan Denisovich*, trans. Ralph Parker (New York: Signet Classics, 1962).

17. Rob Goffee and Gareth Jones, "The Olympics' Greatest Feat: An Unpaid, Highly Engaged Workforce," *Harvard Business Review*, HBR Blog Network, August 8, 2012, https://hbr.org/2012/08/unpaid-and-highly-engaged-the.

Chapter 6

1. Simon Collinson and Melvin Jay, "Complexity Kills Profits," *European Business Review*, November 24, 2011, http://www.europeanbusinessreview.com/?p=3105.

2. July 9, 1970, "Key Speech," http://publications.arup.com/Publications/O/Ove_Arups_Key_Speech.aspx, now widely held by insiders as the Arup corporate bible.

3. Patty McCord, "How Netflix Reinvented HR," *Harvard Business Review*, January–February 2014.

4. Zhang Ruimin, "Raising Haier," *Harvard Business Review*, February 2007.

5. Alvin W. Gouldner, *Patterns of Industrial Bureaucracy* (New York: Free Press 1954).

6. "Hewlett-Packard Rethinks Itself," *Business Week*, April 1, 1991.

7. Talcott Parsons, *The Social System* (New York: Free Press 1951).

8. W. Ong, *Orality and Literacy*, 2nd ed. (New York: Routledge, 2002).

9. "BBC Accused of Snouts-in-the-Trough Culture over Managers' Payoffs," *The Guardian*, July 10, 2013, http://www.theguardian.com/media/2013/jul/10/bbc-accused-snouts-trough-payouts-mps; and "BBC Boss Accused of Presiding over 'Corporate Fraud and Cronyism' Quits," *The Guardian*, August 29, 2013, http://www.theguardian.com/media/2013/aug/29/bbc-human-resources-quits-lucy-adams.

10. Adam Bryant, "In a Corporate Culture, It's a Gift to Be Simple," *New York Times*, November 22, 2013, B2.

11. Adam Bryant, "Intellectual Honesty Is the Best Policy," *New York Times*, March 28, 2014, B2.

Chapter 7

1. Kathleen M. Eisenhardt and Donald Sull, "Strategy as Simple Rules," *Harvard Business Review*, January 2001.

2. Zoë Corbyn, "Is San Francisco Losing Its Soul?" *The Guardian*, February 23, 2014, http://www.theguardian.com/world/2014/feb/23/is-san-francisco-losing-its-soul.

3. Supercell corporate web site; http://supercell.com/en/.

4. "Purpose and Values," Barclays, www.barclays.com/about-barclays/barclays-values.html.

5. A. T. Kearney section based on interviews with Phil Morgan and Gary Singer, and on the company publication "The A.T. Kearney Story" (November 2014).

6. See https://www.atkearney.com/about-us/our-story/a.t.-kearney-story.

7. Henry Mintzberg, "Rebuilding Companies as Communities," *Harvard Business Review*, July–August 2009.

8. Stefan Thomke, "Mumbai's Models of Service Excellence," *Harvard Business Review,* November 2012.

9. Simon Bowers, Guy Grandjean, Phil Maynard, and Alex Purcell, "EY Whistleblower Speaks Out on Conflict Gold Risks," *The Guardian*, February 25, 2014.

10. "Captain Planet," *Harvard Business Review,* June 2012.

Conclusion

1. Amitai Etzioni, *Modern Organizations* (Princeton, NJ: Prentice-Hall, 1964).

Index

Index

Index

Index

Nike, 15
9/11 attacks, 55
Northern Rock, 102
Notter, Jamie, 53
Novartis, 43, 45, 167
Novo Nordisk, 43, 172, 173
  adding value at, 186
  audits at, 118, 179
  communication at, 57, 68
  difference at, 185
  in high-trust society, 192
  sense of identity and history at,
    106–107
  support from the top at, 184
  triple-bottom-line reporting at, 69,
    95, 96

Occupy Wall Street movement,
  160
The Office (TV show), 125
O'Leary, Michael, 114–115
onboarding, 31–32
operational freedom, 158–159
Oraflex, 10, 185
organic solidarity, 24, 47
organizational structure
  around enthusiasms, 138–142
  authority in, 152–153
  communication in, 66
  complexity in, 149–150
  connections and, 129–130
  cultural barriers in, 85–86
  for difference, 23, 42–44
  division and integration through,
    149
  matrix, 62, 130
  radical honesty and, 62
  to support authenticity, 182
organization man, 3, 7, 132
The Organization Man (White), 34

organizations
  contracts with, 5, 7
  creating attachment to,
    131–133
  as determinants of healthy
    societies and lives, 197–198
  freedom maximization in, 8
  as human activity, 7–8
  ideal, 10–13
  identity and roots of, 16, 103–107
  problems with life in, 3–4
  reasons for working in, 8–10
  satisfaction from working in,
    7–8
Øvlisen, Mads, 57
Oxfam, 33
Oxford English Dictionary, 103

Paananen, Ilkka, 23, 175, 179, 191
pain avoidance, 122–123
Parmalat, 102
Parsons, Talcott, 160
particularistic societies, 160
part-time employment, 132–133
passion, 11, 28, 107–111, 138–142
paternalism, 57
Patterns of Industrial Bureaucracy
  (Gouldner), 156–157
pensions, 6–7, 133
PeopleCom, 68
performance
  cultures of, 2
  development for weaker
    performers and, 89, 91–93
  drivers of, 183, 184–187
  engagement and, 11–12
  evaluation of, 155
  impact of complexity on, 149–150
  as motive for working in an
    organization, 9

Index

Acknowledgments

Over the course of almost thirty years, our research has been concerned with two major themes: organizational culture and leadership. The former concern arose from an observation that the old integrators—structures, hierarchies, and careers—were becoming weaker and culture more important; and the latter from a profound dissatisfaction with predominantly psychological approaches to the study of leadership.

To both these areas we have attempted to bring a more distinctively sociological perspective, focusing on the relational aspects of leadership and rescuing the concept of authenticity from an obsession with self-awareness.

Our practical and research involvement in organizations has been driven by two central questions that became the titles of two of our most widely read articles: "What Holds the Modern Company Together?" (*Harvard Business Review*, November–December 1996), subsequently expanded in our book, *The Character of a Corporation*, 1998; and "Why Should Anyone Be Led by You?" (*Harvard Business Review*, September–October 2000), subsequently developed into a book of the same title (Harvard Business School Press, 2006).

More recently, we became interested in the peculiar challenges of leadership in knowledge-intensive economies and wrote about this in our article "Leading Clever People" (*Harvard Business Review*, March 2007) and in a subsequent book, *Clever* (Harvard Business Review Press, 2009).

What links these publications is our continuing interest in what it takes to be an authentic leader. But when some executives explained to us that they would act as authentic leaders when they felt they worked in authentic organizations, we were inevitably driven to a third question and the title of this book, *Why Should Anyone Work Here?*

We have posed this question to hundreds of individuals in different organizations all over the world. They have given of their time to talk with us, to fill in questionnaires, to engage with us in workshops, and to help us build case studies. We are immensely grateful for their generosity and thoughtfulness. We could not have written the book without them. Our thanks go, in particular, to the following organizations: Arup, LOCOG, New York Life, Vestergaard Frandsen, Heineken, A. T. Kearney, LVMH, Waitrose, Novo Nordisk, Ernst & Young, McDonald's, House of St Barnabus, Barclays, Samsung, Sonae, Medicover, Supercell, Unilever, Credit Suisse, Roche, and Nestlé.

As always, we have tested our ideas along the way with colleagues and executives at London Business School and IE Business School, Madrid.

At Harvard Business Review Press, we would like to thank Andrea Ovans, who edited our original article, "Creating the Best Workplace on Earth" (*Harvard Business Review*, May 2013), with passion and dedication. Jeff Kehoe, who has been our book editor for many years, has been, as always, supportive, relentlessly clever, and wise. Liz Baldwin and Sally Ashworth have been bundles of creative energy and always great fun. Lucy McCauley has enthusiastically helped to craft our words and ideas. Pamela McIntyre has kept multiple drafts in order, tolerated our mood swings and obsessions, and listened patiently to our debates about content.

Our families, now habituated to our intense periods of writing and fieldwork, have been endlessly supportive, as always.

About the Authors

Rob Goffee and **Gareth Jones** are Europe's leading experts on organizational culture, leadership, and change. They are past winners of the prestigious McKinsey Award for the best article in *Harvard Business Review*, "Why Should Anyone Be Led by You?" The huge interest it generated led to a five-year journey exploring authentic leadership. Their book of the same title was the culmination of that research and was published by Harvard Business School Press in 2006. In 2008 their article "Leading Clever People" won a second-place McKinsey Award, and was expanded into a book, *Clever*, in 2009.

Rob Goffee is Emeritus Professor of Organisational Behaviour at London Business School, where he teaches in the world-renowned Senior Executive Program. An internationally respected teacher and facilitator, Rob has taught executives from some of the world's leading companies, including Nestlé, LVMH, Roche, and Arup. He also consults to the boards of a number of FTSE 100 companies.

Gareth Jones is a visiting professor at Spain's IE Business School in Madrid and a fellow of the Centre for Management Development at London Business School. In a career that has uniquely spanned both the academic and the business worlds, Gareth was director of human resources and internal communications at the British Broadcasting Corporation (BBC); and at Polygram, then the world's largest recorded music company, he was senior vice president for global human resources. Gareth has worked extensively in high-tech companies, in professional services, notably with PwC, in global fast moving consumer goods companies and widely in the creative industries.

Rob and Gareth are the authors of *The Character of a Corporation* (1998), *Why Should Anyone Be Led by You?* (2006), and *Clever* (2009). Their most recent *Harvard Business* Review article, "Creating the Best Workplace on Earth," was published in December 2013. They are the founding partners of Creative Management Associates, an organizational consulting firm in London. They can be reached at creativemanagementassociates.com.